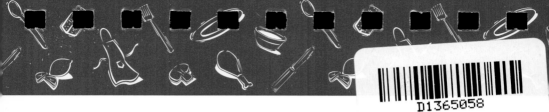

LIST OF RECIP[...]

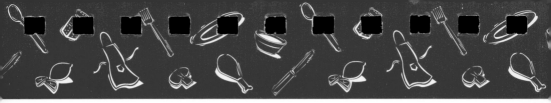

BIRDS AND THINGS WITH HOOVES

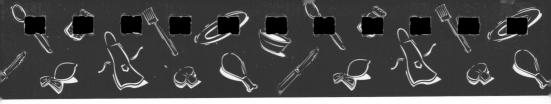

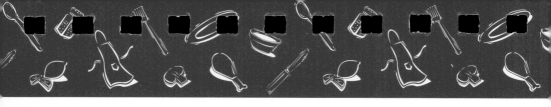

THE FIRE

LAYING YOUR FIRE

My first rule when laying a fire is not to skimp on the fuel. The extra buck you may spend to use the correct amount of fuel will be well worth it in the end. Like having a large grill, having plenty of coals allows you that extra maneuverability that makes grilling easier.

Keeping this in mind, lay a fire with a slightly larger surface area than that of the food you are going to cook, and make it about four inches thick. Then lay a section next to it about half that area—two inches thick. This will give you fairly large surface areas with differing temperatures. Then you will have plenty of room to move food around when it is cooking too fast or too slow, as well as to avoid the frequent flare-ups that occur during grilling.

Remember, this suggestion is a general guideline. If your grill is too small to allow you to build a fire of this size, just build a fire that is at least as large in area as the surface area of the food you are cooking, and make sure that a good portion of the fire—let's say a third—has considerably less fuel than the rest.

IS IT READY YET?

Whichever method you use to light the fire, you should not start cooking until the coals are all uniformly gray. If you want a low-temperature fire, it is better to catch the fire on the way down rather than on the way up. Smoke is basically unburned particles of fuel, and therefore the more completely your fuel is ignited, the cleaner a flame you will have.

In any case, once the coals are covered with a fine layer of gray ash, you need to check to make sure that the fire is the temperature needed to cook whatever you are making that day. A good way to test is by holding your hand about five inches above the cooking surface and seeing how long you can hold it there. If you can hold it there for

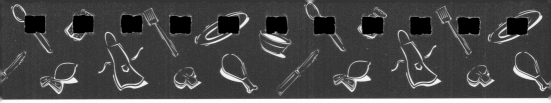

five to six seconds, you have a low fire; three to four seconds is a medium fire; and one to two seconds means you have a hot fire.

You should light your coals about thirty-five to forty minutes before you start cooking if you want a hot fire; forty to forty-five minutes before cooking if you want a medium fire; and forty-five to fifty minutes before cooking if you want a low fire. Each recipe that requires a fire has a temperature bar that indicates how hot a fire is needed.

TOOLS

In addition to the grill and the fuel, you will need a few simple tools for grilling. All can be found at your local restaurant supply store, and I recommend that you get them there, since you are more likely to find the heavy-duty type of equipment that makes grilling easier and more carefree.

HEAVY-DUTY, LONG-HANDLED, SPRING-LOADED TONGS: Absolutely the most essential grilling tool, tongs are to the griller what brushes are to a painter.

OFFSET SPATULA: In the restaurant business, an offset spatula is also known as a dogleg spatula. It has a bent neck, which allows you to get under and lift an item on the grill that is not easily handled with tongs—such as a hamburger or a fish fillet.

HEAVY-DUTY, LONG-HANDLED FORK: You don't want to use this fork to move food around on the grill, since piercing things allows juices to escape. However, it is very handy for any number of uses: probing the flesh of chicken or fish to check for doneness; moving the grill surface to add more fuel; and stirring up the coals when you want a hotter fire.

SKEWERS: You can use either disposable wooden or bamboo skewers or metal ones, which are the sturdiest.

WIRE BRUSH: A necessity for the one slightly unpleasant part of grilling: cleaning the grill surface. Nothing ruins the taste of grilled food faster than the added taste of the food previously cooked on that grill. The best time to clean a grill is immediately after you have finished cooking but before the fire has died.

HOW HOT IS HOT?

◆

(RELATIVE HEAT MEASUREMENTS OF CHILE PEPPERS)

Our individual reaction to the heat in a particular chile pepper is a subjective experience. However, the incendiary properties of chile peppers can be rated scientifically. This is done by measuring the amount of capsaicin (the heat-causing property) in each chile pepper using a standard called Scoville units. A Scoville unit is the number of units of water it takes to make a unit of chile pepper lose all traces of heat. For example, it takes between 2,500 and 5,000 units of water to neutralize the heat from one unit of jalapeño. My favorite *capsicum*, the Scotch Bonnet, aka habañero, checks in at a scorching 150,000 to 300,000 Scoville units.

Below is a relative heat scale that was prepared by chile pepper expert Dave DeWitt, editor of the *Whole Chile Pepper* magazine.

CHILE	SCOVILLE UNITS
Bell Pepper/Pimiento/Sweet Banana	0
Cherry/Mexican Bell	100–500
Big Jim/Anaheim/New Mexican #6	500–1,000
Ancho/Pasilla/Poblano	1,000–1,500
Cascabel/Rocotillo	1,500–2,500
Jalapeño	2,500–5,000
Serrano	5,000–15,000
De Árbol	15,000–30,000
Piquin/Cayenne/Tabasco	30,000–50,000
Aji/Chiltepin/Thai	50,000–100,000
Habañero or Scotch Bonnet	150,000–300,000

ENOUGH OF THESE WILL MAKE A MEAL

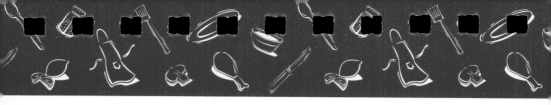

TROPICAL GAZPACHO

◆

Just kind of fooling around one day with some underripe mango and pineapple, I came up with this recipe, one of my all-time favorites. It uses a principle common in tropical regions, treating underripe fruits as vegetables. Here I combine tomato juice with papaya and lime juice for a unique and crisp summer soup.

6 cups canned tomato juice
1 cup canned papaya juice (you may substitute pineapple)
2 medium green or underripe mangoes or papayas, diced small
½ medium pineapple, peeled, cored, and diced small
½ red bell pepper, diced small
½ green bell pepper, diced small
½ cup lime juice (about 4 limes)
4 dashes of Tabasco sauce
½ cup chopped cilantro
Salt and freshly cracked black pepper to taste

Combine the tomato and papaya juice in a large bowl. Add the remaining ingredients, stir a few times, cover, and allow to stand in the refrigerator for at least 2 hours—4 to 6 is best—before serving.

SERVES 6

SERVING SUGGESTIONS: Try this with West Indies Breadfruit Salad (recipe 91) and Lime-Marinated Grilled Kingfish with Red Onion and Mango Relish (recipe 21) for an island-theme dinner.

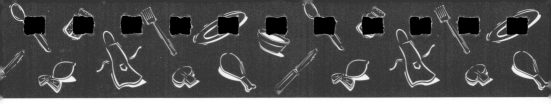

GRILLED VEGETABLE GAZPACHO

◆

In its original days, gazpacho was a bread porridge and not the tomato-vegetable preparation that goes by that name today. Here I restored a little bread for texture, and grilled the vegetables. I like to leave the vegetables in larger pieces rather than chopping them fine, since this gives the soup more textural and taste variety. The char flavor spreads throughout the soup for a very interesting light lunch on a hot day. This is also a good way to use up last night's leftover grilled antipasto.

4 tablespoons olive oil
Salt and freshly cracked black pepper to taste
1 red bell pepper, halved and seeded
1 green bell pepper, halved and seeded
1 small red onion, peeled and halved
½ small eggplant, cut into ½-inch-thick circles

3 garlic cloves
2 slices day-old bread
Salt and freshly cracked black pepper to taste

5 tablespoons olive oil
2 tablespoons balsamic vinegar
1 quart Clamato juice
2 tablespoons chopped fresh basil
4 tablespoons lemon juice (about 1 lemon)

1. Rub the vegetables with 4 tablespoons of olive oil and salt and pepper to taste, and grill them over a medium-hot fire. Grill the peppers and onion for 2 to 3 minutes, turning once or twice, until slightly charred. Then remove them, slice thinly, and set aside. Grill the eggplant circles 2 to 3 minutes per side, until brown, then remove them, cool, and dice small.

2. In a food processor or blender, purée the garlic and bread until fine. Add salt and pepper to taste. With the processor or blender still going, slowly add 5 tablespoons of the oil. Add the balsamic vinegar and blend or process for an additional 15 seconds.

3. Pour the Clamato juice into a large bowl and gradually whisk in the bread mix.

4. Add the grilled vegetables to the Clamato mixture and refrigerate, covered, for 2 to 4 hours.

5. Just before serving, adjust the seasoning with salt and pepper and add the chopped basil and lemon. Mix briefly and serve. Will keep, covered and refrigerated, for 2 to 3 days.

SERVES 6

SERVING SUGGESTIONS: I would serve this with Grilled Lamb Steaks with Rosemary, Garlic, and Red Wine (recipe 41).

GRILLED VEGETABLE ANTIPASTO WITH BRAISED GARLIC BREAD

◆

This dish—the result of my early experiments with the "grillability" of different vegetables at a time when vegetables were not used for grilling—is largely responsible for my reputation for grilling anything and everything. I encourage you to experiment with your favorite vegetables. Make sure they are ultrafresh.

Assembling this antipasto is a lot of fun. Braise the garlic ahead of time, then plan to start cooking this as your guests arrive and let them view all the colors, shapes, and sizes on the grill. It really looks beautiful. Fresh mozzarella or hard provolone makes a smart addition, and adding prosciutto can transform it into a great summer entrée. It's a dish that can sit on a table where people help themselves, and it also makes great leftovers.

8 tablespoons good olive oil
2 garlic cloves, unpeeled
1 summer squash
1 zucchini
1 yellow onion
1 red onion
1 red bell pepper
1 green bell pepper
10 medium mushrooms
Salad oil for rub
Salt and freshly cracked pepper to taste
2 tablespoons balsamic vinegar
8 sun-dried tomatoes
1 cup black olives
2 tablespoons capers
4 tablespoons lemon juice (about 1 lemon)
French or Italian bread

TO BRAISE THE GARLIC
Put 3 tablespoons of the olive oil with the garlic, wrap in foil, and cook in a medium

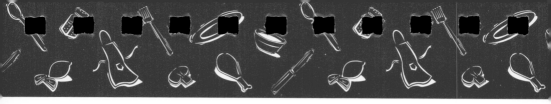

oven (300°F) for ½ hour. The garlic should easily squeeze out of its skin, after which you mix it with the oil in which it was cooked to make a paste. Now you are ready to grill the vegetables.

TO PREPARE THE VEGETABLES

1. Slice the squash and zucchini into ¼-inch rounds.

2. Cut the onions into quarters.

3. Cut the peppers in half and clean out the seeds and membranes.

4. Rub all the vegetables lightly with the salad oil, sprinkle them lightly with salt and pepper to taste, and grill over high heat. What you are looking for here is color. With the exception of the onion, all the vegetables will be cooked properly when the color is right. It's actually fine to have some black parts, because that's the sugar in the vegetables caramelizing, but what you are looking for is really a dark golden brown. Don't overcook them, since you'll want to retain some crispness/rawness in the vegetables to provide texture. The onions require special care: Keep them in quarters and grill them well on the cut sides so that when they are removed from the grill and separated, each piece will have some edges with color and grilled flavor.

5. When the vegetables have achieved the desired state, toss them in balsamic vinegar and 5 tablespoons of the olive oil and arrange them on a platter along with the tomatoes, olives, and capers. Just before serving, squeeze the lemon juice over everything.

6. Cut 4 to 6 chunks of Italian or French bread. If the grill is hot, toast lightly. Be careful, as bread burns easily over an open grill. If the grill is not hot, use the oven to toast the bread. Spread with garlic paste, add to the platter with vegetables, and chomp.

1 LARGE APPETIZER PLATE FOR 4 TO 6 PEOPLE

SERVING SUGGESTIONS: Team this up with another appetizer for a light dinner. Try Seared Sirloin, Sushi Style (recipe 17), or Wilted Greens with Grilled Lamb and Blue Cheese (recipe 14).

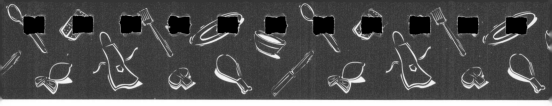

GRILLED EXPENSIVE MUSHROOMS ON TEXAS TOAST

I have always liked the way mushrooms react to the grill, and the abundance of new varieties now commonly available makes experimentation easy. The feature of this dish is the mushrooms themselves, and the way that grilling provides the opportunity for their individual flavors and textures to be displayed. I season them with a touch of sherry and some butter and serve them on top of a slightly seasoned garlic bread to soak up the juices.

1 pound mixed mushrooms (the bigger the
  better)
8 tablespoons olive oil
1 teaspoon freshly cracked black pepper
2 tablespoons unsalted butter, room
  temperature
2 tablespoons sherry
2 tablespoons chopped parsley
Salt and freshly cracked black pepper to taste

1. Wipe the dirt off the mushrooms with a slightly damp cloth or paper towel, and cut off the bottom third of the stems.

2. In a large stainless steel bowl, combine the mushrooms, olive oil, and teaspoon of freshly cracked black pepper. Toss until the mushrooms are well coated with oil—all of the oil should be absorbed.

3. Grill the mushrooms over medium heat, turning occasionally, until brown and crispy, about 8 to 10 minutes.

4. Remove the mushrooms from the grill, slice them into small pieces, and return them to the stainless steel bowl. Add the butter, sherry, and parsley, and toss until the butter has melted.

5. Season with salt and serve on Texas Toast.

SERVES 4 AS AN APPETIZER

TEXAS TOAST

Grilled crusty bread became known as "Texas toast" because people used to think that only cowpokes on the trail would resort to grilling bread over an open fire rather than using an electric toaster. Just goes to show how much we've learned lately.

4 1-inch-thick slices of Italian bread
4 tablespoons olive oil
1 tablespoon minced garlic

Toast the bread in a low oven until hard and crispy. Combine the oil and garlic into a paste, and coat the bread lightly with it.

4 PORTIONS

STEAMED CLAMS WITH LEMON-GRASS AND CHILES DE ÁRBOL

◆

Thailand has some of the best seafood I've ever tasted, which may partially be due to the fact that in Bangkok restaurants the seafood is kept alive in tanks until the moment of preparation. While I think that seafood usually calls for rather subtle flavor combinations that will not overburden the fish, in Thailand I found cooks who could apply highly aromatic, hot preparations to seafood without burying the flavor. (I should note, however, that what is subtle heat to some Thai folks might seem like molten lava to some Western diners.) I think that this combination soup/clam dish works in that way. The broth is great, and I would garnish it with some chopped peanuts and fresh mint.

2 dozen littleneck clams
2 tablespoons minced fresh lemongrass, or 2
    teaspoons dried (see Pantry)

½ head Chinese (Napa) cabbage, thinly sliced
1 cup dry white wine
1 cup bottled clam juice
½ tablespoon minced garlic
2 tablespoons dried chiles de árbol (see Pantry)
    (you may substitute red pepper flakes)
8 tablespoons lime juice (about 4 limes)
¼ cup chopped cilantro
2 tablespoons chopped fresh mint
Salt and freshly cracked black pepper to taste
Coarsely chopped roasted, unsalted peanuts for
    garnish
Mint leaves for garnish

1. Wash the clams and place them in a large stockpot with the lemongrass, cabbage, wine, clam juice, garlic, and chile pepper.

2. Cover and cook over medium heat until the clams have opened, about 10 minutes.

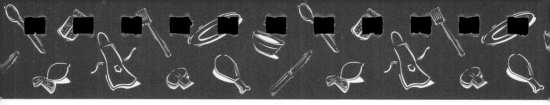

3. Remove them from the heat and add the lime juice, cilantro, chopped mint, and salt and pepper to taste. Swirl around to mix all the ingredients, then serve, garnished with peanuts and mint leaves, in bowls with chunks of bread to soak up the juice.

SERVES 4 AS APPETIZERS

SERVING SUGGESTIONS: Serve this with Grilled Pork Loin with Indonesian Chile-Coconut Sauce (recipe 50) or Grilled Pork Skewers with Green Mango (recipe 51).

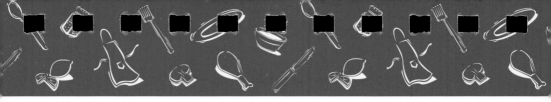

AVOCADO STUFFED WITH SEARED TUNA ESTILIO SEVICHE

This dish was inspired by an evening in Isla Mujeres, an island off the Yucatán in Mexico. I had been shopping for a Panama hat, which I discovered was available in a number of different styles, or estilios—Estilio Al Capone, Estilio Gary Cooper, etc. While wearing my hat Estilio Hoagy Carmichael, I went to a beachfront stand, a *palapa*, and had some great seviche.

Classically, the seviche method—using the acidity of lime or lemon juice to cook fish—is used with raw seafood. Here the tuna is half cooked first. This gives you a concentration of grilled flavor on the cooked side, then the remaining raw part of the fish cooks in the lime juice. I like the contrast of the sharpness of the acid-marinated tuna with the mellowness of the avocado.

1 pound 2-inch-thick tuna steak
8 tablespoons lime juice (about 4 limes)
1 tomato, chopped into large chunks
1 medium red onion, diced small
1 red bell pepper, finely chopped
2 tablespoons chopped cilantro
2 tablespoons extra virgin olive oil
Salt and freshly cracked black pepper to taste
2 ripe avocados, halved, pitted, and peeled
½ medium head green cabbage, very thinly sliced
3 radishes, finely sliced, for garnish
1 lime, cut into rounds, for garnish

1. Over an extra-hot fire, sear the tuna until well-browned on both sides. Make sure your fire is very hot, and grill the tuna very quickly, maximum 2 to 3 minutes per side. You're looking for very high color on the outside, but with the tuna still raw on the inside.

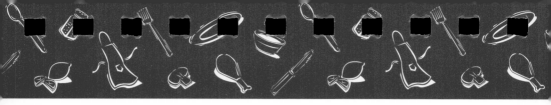

2. Remove the tuna from the grill, let it cool, then slice it into ¼-inch slices.

3. Lay the sliced tuna in a shallow pan, cover it with lime juice, and allow it to sit for 2 to 3 hours.

4. Sprinkle the tomato, onion, pepper, cilantro, and olive oil over the tuna. Season it with salt and black pepper to taste, and toss lightly.

5. Place the avocado halves on a bed of the sliced cabbage. Put 2 to 3 slices of tuna on each avocado half, and spoon any remaining tomato-pepper mixture on top.

6. Sprinkle the radish slices over the tuna, and garnish the platter with the lime rounds.

SERVES 4 AS AN APPETIZER

SERVING SUGGESTIONS: Serve this with Grilled Chicken Breast with Fresh Herbs and Lemon (recipe 57) for dinner.

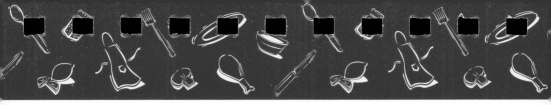

GRILLED SHRIMP WITH SWEET ASIAN CARROT RELISH AND PANCAKES

This dish is loosely based on a Vietnamese-style spring roll. The combination of herbs and peanuts with a sweet carrot relish makes an interesting array of tastes and textures. If you are near an Asian market you will be able to find the rice flour pancakes called for here, but flour tortillas, which are easier to find, are fine.

This is a dish in which your guests get to assemble their own shrimp rolls. I would set everything up in small bowls and let them go at it. Be careful of the chili-garlic condiment—it's superhot.

FOR THE RELISH
2 cups shredded carrots
½ cup rice wine vinegar
2 tablespoons sugar

24 16/20 count (medium-size) shrimp
Salt and freshly cracked pepper (white is best if you have it)

FOR GARNISHES
½ cup coarsely chopped roasted, unsalted peanuts
¼ cup chopped cilantro
¼ cup chopped fresh basil
¼ cup chopped fresh mint
2 tablespoons Vietnamese chili garlic paste (you may substitute 2 tablespoons of a mixture of: 1 tablespoon of your favorite fresh hot chile peppers, finely chopped, 1 tablespoon minced garlic, 1 teaspoon sugar, and 1 tablespoon ketchup)

12 8-inch store-bought rice flour pancakes or flour tortillas, warmed slightly in the oven

1. Combine all the carrot relish ingredients, mix well, and allow the mixture to stand for at least 1 hour before serving. (This relish can easily be made ahead, and will keep, covered and refrigerated, for 2 to 3 days.)

2. Peel and devein the shrimp, and remove the tails. Thread them on skewers, season them with salt and pepper to taste, and grill them over medium heat, 3 to 4 minutes per side. Remove and set them aside.

3. When the shrimp are cool, chop them coarsely in 2 or 3 pieces each.

4. Put the shrimp, relish, garnishes, and warm pancakes or tortillas out in the middle of the table, and let your guests make their own little spring rolls.

SERVES 6 AS AN APPETIZER

SERVING SUGGESTIONS: Serve this as an appetizer in front of Grilled Pork Loin with Indonesian Chile-Coconut Sauce (recipe 50) or Grilled Pork Skewers with Green Mango (recipe 51).

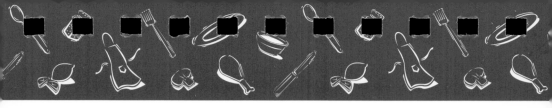

GRILLED SHRIMP WITH PINEAPPLE-ANCHO CHILE SALSA AND TORTILLAS

This is one of your basic guest participation dishes, calling for folks to create according to their own taste.

I first tasted pineapple and cilantro in a salsa in San Blas, on the west coast of Mexico, which possesses some of the best shrimp I ever ate, as well as the longest rideable wave in Mexico. Taking breathers from many hours in the water, we would come up to a *palapa* (a beachfront stand) to eat bowlfuls of shrimp and drink beer.

You can serve the shrimp in a heap with piles of chopped onion and thinly sliced cabbage. You have to have fresh, soft tortillas and just slap them on the grill for a second to warm them up.

24 16/20 count (medium-size) shrimp
Salt and freshly cracked black pepper to taste

FOR THE SALSA
½ ripe medium pineapple
½ red bell pepper
½ large red onion
4 ancho chile peppers, soaked in water for 12 hours, drained, and pureed
1 tablespoon chopped fresh oregano
1 teaspoon ground cumin
6 tablespoons lime juice (about 3 limes)
¼ cup pineapple juice
16 soft tortillas (flour or corn), warmed slightly in the oven

FOR THE GARNISHES
½ head green or red cabbage, shredded
½ cup sour cream
¼ cup chopped fresh red or green jalapeño chile
* peppers*

1. Peel and devein the shrimp and remove their tails.

2. Thread the shrimp on skewers, salt and pepper them to taste, and grill over medium heat, 3 to 4 minutes per side, until they are opaque.

3. Remove the shrimp from the skewers and chop each shrimp into 3 or 4 pieces. Set aside.

4. Make the salsa: Dice the pineapple, red pepper, and red onion. Add the puréed ancho chile peppers, and mix together in a medium bowl with the oregano, cumin, and lime and pineapple juices.

5. Warm the tortillas slightly on the grill.

6. Put the shrimp, salsa, and tortillas out on a table, along with the shredded cabbage, sour cream, and jalapeños as garnishes, and let people make their own tortillas.

SERVES 4 AS AN APPETIZER

SERVING SUGGESTIONS: Serve this with Grilled Pork Birdies with Tangerine-Rosemary Glaze (recipe 53) or Grilled Lime-Marinated Flank Steak with Chipotle-Honey Sauce (recipe 46). It would also make a nice, light summer dinner in combination with Caribbean-Style Grilled Seafood Soup (recipe 34).

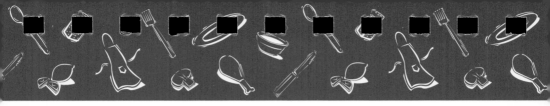

GRILLED AND CHILLED SHRIMP WITH CABBAGE AND PEANUTS

This is perfect for a lunch entrée on a hot summer day or a first course at dinner. The lightness, freshness, and aromaticity of the typical Thai/Southeast Asian herb combination go very well with the shrimp.

16 16/20 count (medium-size shrimp)
Salt and freshly cracked black pepper to taste (white is best, if you have it)
1 small head green cabbage
½ cup rice wine vinegar
¼ cup roasted, unsalted peanuts, coarsely ground
2 tablespoons chopped fresh basil
2 tablespoons chopped fresh cilantro
2 tablespoons very finely minced fresh lemongrass or 2 teaspoons dried lemongrass (see Pantry)
1 teaspoon sugar
2 tablespoons sesame oil
1 teaspoon Vietnamese chili garlic paste (you may substitute 1 teaspoon of a mixture of: 1 tablespoon of your favorite fresh hot chile peppers, finely chopped, mixed with 1 tablespoon minced garlic, 1 teaspoon sugar, and 1 tablespoon ketchup)
4 tablespoons lime juice (about 2 limes)

1. Peel and devein the shrimp and remove their tails.

2. Season the shrimp with salt and pepper to taste, thread them on a skewer and grill them over medium heat until opaque, about 3 to 4 minutes per side.

3. Remove the skewered shrimp from the heat and allow to cool.

4. While the shrimp are cooling, slice the head of the cabbage very thin and, in a large bowl, combine the cabbage with all the remaining ingredients and mix well.

5. Remove the cooled shrimp from the skewers and chop each one into 5 to 6 pieces.

6. Add the chopped shrimp to the other ingredients, toss lightly, and serve at once.

SERVES 4 AS AN APPETIZER

SERVING SUGGESTIONS: Serve this as an appetizer followed by Simple Grilled Whole Beef Tenderloin (recipe 48). If you're serving it as a lunch entrée, accompany it with a bowl of Spicy Cucumber Relish (recipe 74).

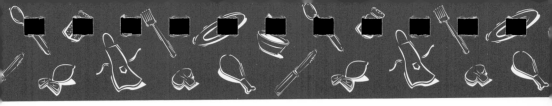

GRILLED SALMON,
LOMI LOMI STYLE

◆

This is a takeoff of sorts on the Hawaiian luau salmon preparation called *lomi lomi*. The difference is that in the preparation, the salmon is not salt-cured, but instead is half cooked on the grill before cooking is completed by the acidity of the lime juice.

This dish illustrates my observation that the natural cuisine of Hawaii is unique among tropical cuisines in all absence of spicy ingredients and preparations. Serve it chilled as a first course on a bed of thinly sliced cabbage with pineapple slices and lime wedges.

*1½ pound center-cut salmon fillet, in 1 or 2
   pieces*
2 tablespoons vegetable oil
Salt and freshly cracked black pepper to taste
¾ cup lime juice (about 6 limes)
½ cup pineapple juice

1 medium red onion, diced small
3 scallions, diced small
2 tablespoons chopped parsley
½ teaspoon Tabasco sauce
½ teaspoon sugar
3 fresh tomatoes, diced small

1. Skin the salmon and, if you have bought one fillet, cut it into 2 pieces. Brush the tops with vegetable oil, sprinkle them with salt and pepper to taste, and place the salmon top down (the side you skinned up) on a very hot grill. Cook for 4 to 5 minutes, until brown and crusty.

2. Remove the salmon from the grill. It should be well cooked on one side, but still raw on the other. Allow it to cool to room temperature.

3. Meanwhile, combine all the other ingredients except the tomato in a large mixing bowl and mix well.

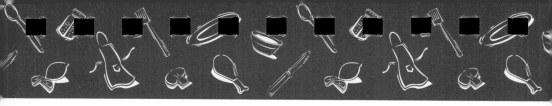

4. When the salmon is cool, break it into bite-size pieces and add them to the lime juice mixture, cooked-side up. Stir lightly to make sure that all the pieces are well coated, then cover tightly and refrigerate for 4 to 5 hours.

5. Remove the bowl from the refrigerator and add the chopped tomatoes. You can serve this chilled or at room temperature.

SERVES 6 AS AN APPETIZER

SERVING SUGGESTIONS: Try this in front of Seared Sirloin, Sushi Style (recipe 17).

GRILLED CHICKEN
DRUMSTICKS BERBERÉ

Berberé is the name of a peppery spice paste that is a staple in Ethiopian cooking. It can contain any number of spices, and I'm sure that in Ethiopia cooks argue the merits of their own particular blend. My recipe is one of the many variations but retains the classic Ethiopian method of pan-cooking the spices to bring out their flavor, and of course I would not be true to the dish if I made it any less hot than the original. File this one under "Wicked Hot" and make sure to have some cold ones on ice.

1 teaspoon powdered ginger
1 tablespoon red pepper flakes
1 teaspoon ground cardamom
2 teaspoons ground coriander
1 tablespoon star anise, crushed
1 teaspoon turmeric
1 tablespoon dry mustard
1 teaspoon fenugreek seeds, crushed (optional)

1 teaspoon nutmeg
1 teaspoon cinnamon
1 teaspoon allspice
2 tablespoons cayenne pepper
1 tablespoon freshly cracked black pepper
2 tablespoons salt
½ cup paprika
½ cup dry red wine
4 tablespoons peanut oil
¼ cup fresh orange juice
16 chicken drumsticks
Lemons for squeezing

1. Combine all the dry spices, from the ginger through paprika, in a bowl and mix well.

2. In a large sauté pan, cook the combined spices over medium heat for 2 to 3 minutes, until they are heated completely through. Be careful of the fumes—the spice aroma is very strong and quite bizarre.

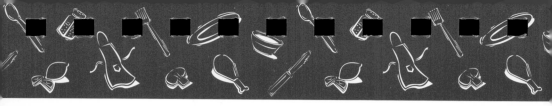

Your house will smell like a Moroccan *souk* (market) even if you use the fan.

3. Add the red wine to the spice mixture and cook 2 to 3 minutes, stirring constantly, until a uniform paste is formed.

4. Remove the spice paste from the heat and allow it to cool. Add the peanut oil and orange juice and mix well. The paste should have the consistency of wet sand.

5. Rub the drumsticks all over with the berberé mixture and allow them to stand, covered, in the refrigerator for 2 hours.

6. Grill the drumsticks over medium-low heat for 10 to 12 minutes, rolling them around to ensure even coloring. Check for doneness by nicking the largest one at its thickest point. The meat should be fully opaque with no traces of red.

7. Remove the drumsticks from the heat and serve them at once with lemons for squeezing and plenty of cold beer.

SERVES 8 AS AN APPETIZER

SERVING SUGGESTIONS: Try these in front of Grilled Peppered Wolffish (recipe 19).

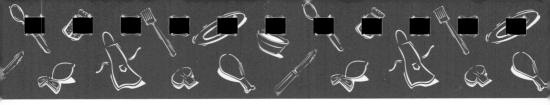

GRILLED BASQUE WINGS

◆

These wings are great to gnaw on while you're diligently grilling the main course and sipping a cold one, as my Basque friend Juan Riesco often demonstrated to me. The level of heat is up to you—the Tabasco is your fuel.

3 large garlic cloves, chopped
8 tablespoons lemon juice (about 2 lemons)
2 tablespoons virgin olive oil
5 to 15 dashes of Tabasco sauce, depending on your taste
3 tablespoons chopped fresh herbs (whatever you've got: basil, parsley, sage, thyme, oregano, or rosemary)
20 chicken wings (you can usually get a pack of wings at the market very cheap)
Salt and freshly cracked black pepper to taste

1. In a large serving bowl, mix together all the ingredients, except the chicken wings.

2. You will notice that the wing has two joints. Cut through both joints, separating the wing into three pieces. The wing tip is not usable here, so either toss it out or freeze it and throw it into your next stock, a purpose for which it is excellent.

3. Salt and pepper the wing pieces to taste and whip them onto a medium-hot grill. Turn them occasionally until golden brown, about 5 minutes. To see if they're done, take a big one off the grill and bite into it.

4. When the wings are cooked through, add them to the bowl with the dressing and mix to thoroughly cover. Set them on a platter, open a cold beer, and enjoy yourself.

SERVES 4 TO 6 AS AN APPETIZER

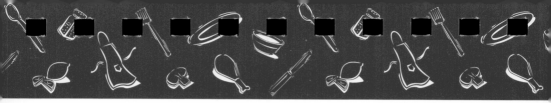

SERVING SUGGESTIONS: These are excellent "tapas"-style appetizers. Serve them at a large cocktail party along with some other Mediterranean-inspired appetizer such as Grilled Steamed Littlenecks Johnson (recipe 31).

When separating chicken wings, at first you will probably want to use a cleaver. With a little practice, however, you will easily find the weak spot in the joint every time and graduate to using a sharp knife.

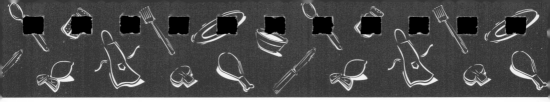

GRILLED CHICKEN THIGHS WITH PEACH, BLACK OLIVE, AND RED ONION RELISH

MEDIUM-LOW

I think the contrasting flavors of ripe fruit and black olives meld together very well. The earthy Kalamatas add just a trace of bitterness against the sweetness of the fruit. Combine these tastes with the distinctive flavor of grilled chicken, and you have a dish simple to prepare with a wide range of flavors competing for your attention but not getting out of hand. Sort of like having dinner with a well-behaved family group. I use chicken thighs here because the meat has more flavor than the breast does and the pieces are smaller and therefore easier to grill without burning.

3 ripe peaches
½ cup fresh black Kalamata olives (you may substitute any fresh black olives, but do not use canned)
1 small red onion, diced small
1 roasted red pepper, diced small (see Pantry)
4 tablespoons extra virgin olive oil
2 tablespoons balsamic vinegar
1 teaspoon minced garlic
1 tablespoon fresh thyme
Salt and freshly cracked black pepper to taste
4 tablespoons lemon juice (about 1 lemon)
8 chicken thighs

1. Pit the peaches and cut them into pieces about the size of sugar cubes. Pit the olives and cut them in half.

2. Combine the peaches, olives, and red pepper in a mixing bowl.

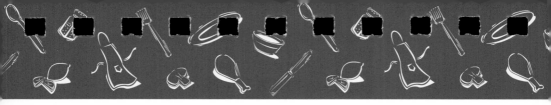

3. Add the olive oil, vinegar, garlic, and thyme, and toss lightly. Add salt and pepper to taste.

4. Cover the mixture and allow it to stand at room temperature for at least 1 hour. It will keep, covered in the refrigerator, for up to 3 days, if you want to make it ahead, although this additional time won't change the flavor for better or worse.

5. Just before serving, add the lemon juice and mix lightly.

6. Season the chicken thighs with salt and pepper to taste. Grill skin-side down over medium-low heat, 8 to 10 minutes, or until the skin is crispy. Flip them over and cook an additional 4 to 6 minutes. To make sure they are fully done, make an incision close to the bone and look for redness, which you don't want. Serve them warm or cold with peach relish.

SERVES 8 AS AN APPETIZER

SERVING SUGGESTIONS: Try this as a main course with Your Basic Grilled Corn (recipe 96).

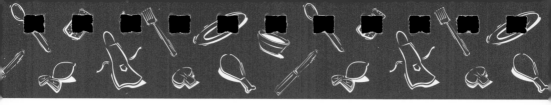

WILTED GREENS WITH GRILLED LAMB AND BLUE CHEESE

◆

Although this dish may seem a little "out there," I encourage you to try it. The combination of bitter greens and blue cheese is outstanding, and the grilled lamb provides a distinct texture and flavor. I like to use dandelion greens, but others will suffice. Avoid kale or collard greens, though, because you won't have enough time to tenderize them. Use a combination of 3 parts spinach greens to 1 part mustard, beet, or turnip greens if no dandelions are available.

1 pound lamb from the leg, cut into ½-inch
*   cubes*
Salt and freshly cracked black pepper to taste
4 tablespoons olive oil
2 pounds dandelion greens, separated,
*   washed, and dried*
4 tablespoons balsamic vinegar
Pinch of sugar
6 ounces blue cheese, crumbled

1. Season the lamb cubes with salt and pepper to taste, thread them on skewers, and grill over high heat for 3 to 4 minutes per side. The lamb should remain pink inside.

2. In a large sauté pan, heat the oil until very hot but not smoking, then add the greens. Turn them furiously with tongs while you count to five, being sure to coat them all with oil.

3. Remove the greens from the heat to a bowl, and continue mixing until they are bright green or wilted. Add the vinegar and sugar, salt and pepper to taste, and toss well.

4. Spoon out the greens mixture onto 4 individual plates, place the cubes of grilled lamb on top, and sprinkle generously with the crumbled blue cheese.

SERVES 4 AS AN APPETIZER

GRILLED TOAST
CANAPÉ VARIATIONS

◆

These canapés are perfect for cocktail parties. The grilled bread makes them rather special, and when you put them on a platter together they look like a huge sea of different colors, shapes, and textures. I have given some ideas here, but these canapés are an excellent vehicle for using leftovers. Use your imagination. The only principle is that each one should have a strong flavor.

1 cup olive oil
2 tablespoons minced garlic
1 fresh baguette, cut into ¼-inch slices
   (about 40)
Olive oil
Balsamic vinegar

1. Combine the 1 cup olive oil and the garlic and, using a brush, paint both sides of each slice of bread with this mixture.

2. Over a low fire, grill the bread slices on both sides until golden brown and crisp, about 1 minute per side.

3. Arrange items from last night's grilled feast or your favorite local store on top of the bread slices. You might use grilled mushrooms with parsley; roasted red peppers with fresh mozzarella; goat cheese and sun-dried tomatoes; cucumbers chopped with tomatoes, lemon, and herbs; grilled eggplant with grated pecorino cheese; anchovies chopped with bread crumbs and capers; prosciutto with olive oil; grilled onions and chopped fresh oregano. Arrange the canapés on a large platter, and drizzle olive oil and balsamic vinegar over all.

ABOUT 40 CANAPÉS

PASTA FROM HELL

Constantly challenged by my fire-eating customers to create hotter and hotter food, I decided to put a stop to it once and for all by developing a dish that would satisfy their desires and quiet their demands. A dish so hot that there was no hotter; so hot that never again would I have to take a ribbing from the heat freaks.

This is it. Your heat source here is the Scotch Bonnet chile pepper, widely accepted as the hottest commercially cultivated chile pepper in the world. Many of my customers think this dish is just a bit too much, Kitchen Out of Control. But a handful of others, with sweat coming off the tops of their heads, eyes as big as saucers, bathed in satanic ecstasy, tell me that it's the best thing I've ever created. The truth lies somewhere in the middle, and in fact the heat in this dish can be controlled by using far fewer peppers without impairing the flavor of the dish. But...every once in a while, when the really hard case sits down and insists on something that has a "real kick" to it, whip the full-bore Pasta from Hell on him. We're talking culinary respect here.

2 tablespoons olive oil
1 yellow onion, diced small
1 red bell pepper, diced small
2 bananas, sliced
¼ cup pineapple juice
Juice of 3 oranges
4 tablespoons lime juice (about 2 limes)
¼ cup chopped cilantro
3 to 4 tablespoons finely chopped fresh red or green hot chile peppers (Scotch Bonnet or Habañero is best) or 4 to 6 ounces Inner Beauty Hot Sauce (see Pantry)
About ¼ cup grated Parmesan cheese
2 teaspoons unsalted butter
1 pound fettuccine
Salt and freshly cracked black pepper to taste

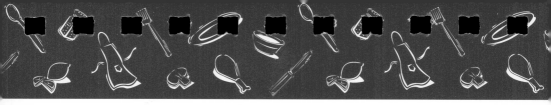

1. In a large saucepan, heat the oil and sauté the onion and red pepper in it over medium heat for about 4 minutes.

2. Add the bananas and pineapple and orange juice. Simmer over medium heat for 5 minutes, until the bananas are soft.

3. Remove from the heat, add the lime juice, cilantro, chile peppers, or Inner Beauty sauce, and 3 tablespoons of the Parmesan cheese, and mix well.

4. In 4 quarts of boiling salted water, cook the fettuccine until al dente, about 8 to 10 minutes for dried pasta, 3 to 4 for fresh. Drain and put it into a stainless steel bowl.

5. Add the spicy mixture, butter, and mix well. Season with salt and pepper to taste and garnish with the remaining Parmesan.

SERVES 4 AS AN APPETIZER

SERVING SUGGESTIONS: Serve this with East Coast Grill Corn Bread (recipe 99) to serve as a fire extinguisher.

SEARED SIRLOIN, SUSHI STYLE

For those who like steak tartare and carpaccio, an Asian-inspired addition to the raw beef dish line. Rubbed with spices, the steak is then cooked quickly at a high heat, concentrating flavor on the seared surface while leaving the interior basically raw. It is served with the traditional Japanese raw fish accompaniments of soy sauce, pickled ginger, and wasabi, a Japanese green horseradish. I always like the combination of rare/raw meat and horseradish, and the sweet ginger smoothes it all out. I rub wasabi on the meat with a little ginger, then roll it up and dunk it in the soy sauce.

SPICE RUB FOR THE STEAK
1 tablespoon freshly cracked white pepper
1 tablespoon freshly cracked black pepper
1 tablespoon kosher salt
1 tablespoon Five Spice Powder (available in Asian markets)
1 tablespoon paprika
1 teaspoon powdered ginger
16- to 20-ounce sirloin steak, 2 inches thick, trimmed of all the fat (let your butcher prepare it)

ACCOMPANIMENTS
½ cup soy sauce
6 ounces pickled ginger (see Pantry)
4 tablespoons wasabi, mixed thoroughly with 4 tablespoons water (see Pantry).

1. Mix the white and black peppers, salt, Five Spice Powder, paprika, and ginger, and rub the steak on all sides with the spice mixture. Allow it to stand, uncovered, at room temperature for 1 hour.

2. Over a very hot fire, heavily sear the steak on all its surfaces, 2 minutes per surface. (You will have four surfaces on a steak this thick: top, bottom, and two sides.) You are looking for a well-browned, thoroughly seared surface, but since you want

the heat to penetrate only the outer layer of the meat, you must be sure to do it at a very high heat.

3. Remove the meat from the grill and allow it to cool at least 20 minutes before serving. If you want, you can refrigerate it, covered, for up to 2 days, and bring it out an hour before serving to remove the chill.

4. Slice the meat paper-thin across the grain and arrange it on a platter with the accompaniments.

SERVES 4 AS AN APPETIZER

SERVING SUGGESTIONS: I would serve this in front of Grilled Bluefish with Chipotle Vinaigrette (recipe 23) or Grilled Pompano with Lime and Olive Oil (recipe 25).

GRILLED SAUSAGE PATTIES WITH CELERIAC AND FENNEL SLAW

When I grew up we had sausage patties only for breakfast. Now, happily, they turn up on lunch and dinner menus. To make these patties, use fresh Italian sweet sausages, slash the casing, and squeeze the meat out. Or, if you prefer, you can simply grill the links. The celeriac and fennel slaw provides a hearty, earthy companion to the Italian theme of the dish.

FOR THE SAUSAGE PATTIES
1 pound fresh Italian sweet link sausages
1 tablespoon minced garlic
1 tablespoon finely chopped fresh basil
1 tablespoon finely chopped fresh rosemary
Salt and freshly cracked black pepper to taste

1. Slash the casings of the sausages and squeeze the meat out into a large bowl. Add all the remaining ingredients, mix very well, and shape into 4 flat patties.

2. Make a hot fire under half the grill. Place the sausage patties over the side without the fire (to avoid constant flare-ups from the high fat content of the sausages) and cook about 10 minutes per side. Check doneness by slicing one of the patties in half like a bun. The meat should be cooked through, a uniform juicy gray. If not done, slice all the patties in this manner and grill raw-side down for 3 more minutes to finish.

3. Remove them from the grill and serve with the slaw, prepared according to the following card.

FOR THE SLAW (ABOUT 4 CUPS)
½ *bulb fresh fennel (about ½ pound),*
   julienned
1 pound celeriac, julienned
1 tablespoon celery seed
2 tablespoons Dijon mustard
½ *cup olive oil*
¾ *cup lemon juice (about 3 lemons)*
2 tablespoons chopped parsley
Salt and freshly cracked black pepper to taste

1. In a large bowl, combine the fennel, celeriac, celery seed, mustard, and olive oil, and mix very well.

2. Add the lemon juice, parsley, and salt and pepper to taste, and toss well.

SERVES 4 AS AN APPETIZER

SERVING SUGGESTIONS: I would serve this dish in front of Spice-Rubbed Grilled Monkfish (recipe 20).

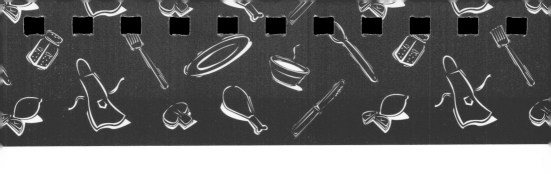

FISH AND OTHER WATER DWELLERS

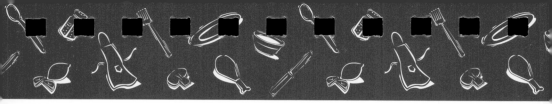

GRILLED PEPPERED WOLFFISH

The wolffish spends most of its time in the North Atlantic just north of Cape Cod, and its season is from fall to spring. Its name comes from its nasty wolflike appearance. It also goes under the more salable name of ocean catfish, because its face vaguely resembles the freshwater catfish. This is not a superpopular fish, although I'm not sure why. It is a lean, mild-tasting white fish with a very firm texture similar to that of monkfish, making it excellent for grilling. It is usually reasonably priced and has the texture and consistency to go well with strong preparations. You can serve this with a fresh mustard or mayonnaise, or with just a squeeze of lemon and a hunk of butter on top.

4 8- to 10-ounce wolffish fillets
4 tablespoons olive oil
½ cup freshly cracked black pepper

1. Rub the fillets all over with the oil, then coat them evenly and heavily with the pepper.

2. Over a hot fire, grill the fillets 5 to 6 minutes per side, until uniformly crusty. Probe the flesh to check for a consistently opaque center, which indicates that the fish is properly cooked. If a proper crust has been obtained but the flesh is underdone, leave the fillets on the grill but move them over to the side so they are not over the flames. Continue to cook them until completely opaque.

SERVES 4 AS A MAIN COURSE

SERVING SUGGESTIONS: In the summer, serve it accompanied by Your Basic Grilled Corn (recipe 96).

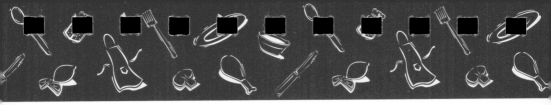

SPICE-RUBBED GRILLED MONKFISH

◆

MEDIUM-HIGH

The slightly sweet, mild monkfish is a fantastic foil for strong preparations, which it can stand up to because of its meaty consistency. This is wonderful with Chipotle Pepper Mayonnaise (recipe 84) served on the side. When you buy monkfish, make sure the tough outer membrane is removed, or you will have some trouble with it.

FOR THE SPICE RUB
¼ cup ground cumin
2 tablespoons paprika
2 tablespoons chili powder
1 tablespoon light brown sugar
1 tablespoon freshly cracked black pepper
1 tablespoon cayenne pepper
2 tablespoons dried oregano

1 2½-pound monkfish fillet

1. Combine all the spice rub ingredients in a bowl, then rub the fillet thoroughly with the mixture.

2. Over a medium-hot fire, grill the monkfish on both sides for a total of about 15 minutes. The fillet will be sort of round, so roll it as opposed to flipping it in order to cook it evenly. Don't worry when the exterior of the fish gets dark brown: This is the result of the spice rub and just indicates that the fish is properly done.

SERVES 4 AS A MAIN COURSE

MARINADES AND GRILLING

Many people advise you to marinate meat and fish before grilling, but I don't usually recommend it.

There are two reasons that people give for marinating—to impart flavor, and to aid in tenderizing. Now, I might occasionally use a marinade to impart flavor, but only when using cuts with a very large surface area, such as flank steak. This is because, in a twenty-four-hour marinating period, the actual penetration of the marinade into the food is minimal, so you really gain nothing but surface flavor. In general, I prefer a dry rub, which not only imparts surface flavor more efficiently, but also aids in the formation of a flavorful crust or sear. Of course, a rub is not practical for all situa-

tions. When it isn't, I prefer to take the flavors I would be adding by marinating, and instead add them after cooking, in the form of a dressing or relish.

As far as tenderizing goes, most meat that is suitable for grilling is tender to begin with, so there is no need for tenderizing. Also, if you are using an acid-based marinade, you actually break down the cell structure of the protein in meat, with the result that the outside of the meat becomes slightly mushy while the interior is unaffected. I suppose this make the meat more palatable to some, but I think the term "tenderizing" in the case of marinades is a bit of a mis-nomer—"surface softening" might be more accurate.

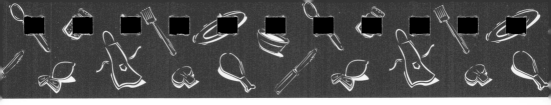

LIME-MARINATED GRILLED KINGFISH WITH RED ONION AND MANGO RELISH

The kingfish, the largest member of the mackerel family, runs in the summer as far north as the Chesapeake Bay, but it mostly resides on the east coast of Florida and the West Indies—smart fish. It is similar to the bluefish in its oily content, but to me has a much more subtle taste. Don't be turned off by either the "oily" quality—think of it as "buttery" and you'll like it a lot better—or by its membership in the mackerel clan. More than one person has thanked me for forcing him to try this fish. Obviously a favorite of mine, this firm-textured fellow is well suited for grilling and has enough taste to stand up to spicy sauces. Putting a pie pan over the fish creates an oven effect that helps cook it through before it burns.

2 pounds kingfish fillets, cut into 8-ounce portions
Salt and freshly cracked black pepper to taste
6 tablespoons lime juice (about 3 limes)
2 tablespoons vegetable oil

1. Place the kingfish skin-side down in a small, flat plastic container or shallow baking pan. You need a container in which the fillets can be packed tightly together, but with their surfaces exposed.

2. Season the fillets with salt and pepper to taste, and pour the lime juice over them. Cover and place them in the refrigerator for 4 to 6 hours.

3. Remove the fillets, pat them dry, and brush them with oil.

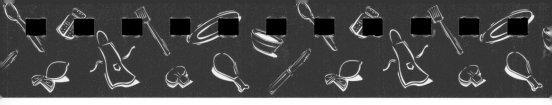

4. Place the fillets skin-side up on the grill over medium heat. Cover them with a pie pan and cook 8 to 10 minutes.

5. Remove the pie pan, flip the fillets, and cook them an additional 5 to 7 minutes. Check to see if they are properly cooked by probing the flesh, looking for a consistent opacity.

6. Serve the fish accompanied by Red Onion and Mango Relish.

SERVES 4 AS A MAIN COURSE

SERVING SUGGESTIONS: Serve this with West Indies Breadfruit Salad (recipe 91).

RED ONION AND MANGO RELISH

1 ripe mango, diced
2 tablespoons chopped cilantro
1 small red onion, diced
1 tablespoon chopped red or green jalapeño chile peppers
3 tablespoons lime juice (about 1½ limes)
2 dashes of Tabasco sauce
Salt and freshly cracked black pepper to taste

Mix all the ingredients together. This relish will keep up to 3 days, covered, in the refrigerator.

ABOUT 1½ CUPS

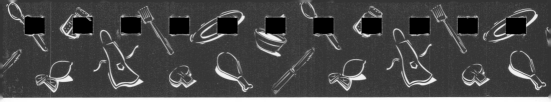

GRILLED HALIBUT STEAKS WITH FRESH TOMATO SAUCE

The halibut is the largest member of the flounder family, sometimes weighing as much as seven hundred pounds. This means that, although it is a flat fish, its body is thick enough to cut steaks from, with the bone in. When grilling, I always prefer fish or meat with bones, since they hold together better, are tenderer, and retain more juice and flavor. The halibut's firm flesh and delicate flavor also make it particularly suitable for grilling.

2 large ripe tomatoes, diced
¼ cup fresh basil, chopped
3 tablespoons extra virgin olive oil
1 tablespoon balsamic vinegar
4 8-ounce halibut steaks
3 tablespoons vegetable oil
Salt and freshly cracked black pepper to taste
4 tablespoons lemon juice (about 1 lemon)
1 teaspoon minced garlic

1. Put the diced tomato into a mixing bowl.

2. Add the basil, olive oil, and vinegar, mix well, and set aside.

3. Rub the fish with vegetable oil and season with salt and pepper to taste. Grill the fish over a medium-hot fire for 5 to 6 minutes per side, until the flesh is opaque all the way through.

4. Add the lemon juice and garlic to the tomato mixture, and mix well. Spoon some sauce on a plate and place a fillet on top of the sauce.

SERVES 4 AS A MAIN COURSE

SERVING SUGGESTIONS: Serve this with Your Basic Grilled Corn (recipe 96).

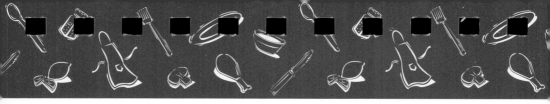

GRILLED BLUEFISH WITH CHIPOTLE VINAIGRETTE

Here you have a very strong, distinct-tasting, oily fish versus a hot, smoky, highly acidic vinaigrette. A great combination, as both flavors will be heard from. This dish can be served warm or cold .

4 tablespoons cider vinegar
1 tablespoon brown prepared mustard
1 tablespoon puréed chipotle pepper
1 teaspoon chopped cilantro
4 tablespoons lime juice (about 2 limes)
1 teaspoon sugar
½ cup extra virgin olive oil
Salt and freshly cracked black pepper to taste
4 8-ounce bluefish fillets
2 tablespoons vegetable oil
Lime halves for garnish
Chopped cilantro for garnish
Chopped red onion for garnish

1. In a small bowl, whisk together the vinegar, mustard, puréed pepper, cilantro, lime juice, and sugar. Add the olive oil, still whisking, until the mixture is well mixed. Add salt and pepper to taste.

2. Season the fillets with salt and pepper to taste and rub with the vegetable oil.

3. Over medium-low heat, place the fillets skin-side up on the grill, and cover them with a pie pan. Cook 10 to 12 minutes, remove the pie pan, and flip the fillets with a spatula. Cook them an additional 5 minutes. Check to see if they're completely done by probing the flesh, looking for consistent opacity.

4. Remove the fillets from the grill, place them on a platter, and pour the vinaigrette over them. Garnish with lime halves, chopped cilantro, and red onion.

SERVES 4 AS A MAIN COURSE

GRILLED WHOLE RED PARTY SNAPPER WITH TWO SAUCES

The red snapper is the king of the tropical sea-dwelling snapper family. This fish runs from the east coast of the United States all the way down to Brazil, and spends a lot of time off the shores of Florida in the Gulf of Mexico. Its distinctive red skin makes a beautiful presentation, and the delicately sweet small flake belies its firm texture. The impressive sight of a whole red snapper cooking on the grill is surpassed only by the sight of that same fish on the plate in front of you, looking festive and delicious. Don't be intimidated by the imagined difficulty of grilling a whole fish. Take it slow and be patient and you won't have any problems. The bones in the fish help keep it moist, and they are not a serious pain to remove.

4 1½ pound whole red snappers, scaled and gutted
4 tablespoons vegetable oil
Salt and freshly cracked black pepper to taste

1. On each fish, make 3 cuts with a knife diagonally along each side, down to the bone. This is done to facilitate cooking and also because it is easier to peek into these gaps to determine doneness.

2. Brush each fish with vegetable oil and season with salt and pepper to taste.

3. Take special care with the fire here, since a whole fish is somewhat tricky to cook all the way through without torching its exterior. Wait until your fire is medium-hot but on the way down to low. This way, the first side of the fish to be cooked will get a nice color coating, while the flip side can stay on the grill long enough to finish cooking at a lower temperature.

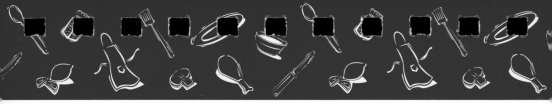

4. Okay, so here we go. Place the fish on the grill and cook them on the first side for 10 to 20 minutes, until well charred. Using your dogleg spatula, flip the fish and continue cooking an additional 12 to 15 minutes. Probe in the slashes to check for doneness—the flesh should be uniformly white. Remove the fish from grill and serve, accompanied by the two salsas.

5. Instruct your guests to remove the top fillet of each fish, then yank the spine from the tail up, removing all bones.

SERVES 4 AS A MAIN COURSE

HOT RED SALSA

*4 large ripe tomatoes (about 1½ pounds),
    cored and coarsely chopped*
½ cup lime juice (about 4 limes)
¼ cup chopped cilantro
1 medium red onion, diced small
*4 small fresh red or green jalapeño chile
    peppers, finely chopped*
Salt and freshly cracked black pepper to taste

Put all the ingredients in a mixing bowl, and mix well. Salsa will keep up to 3 days, covered, in the refrigerator.

ABOUT 2 CUPS

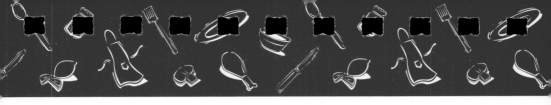

JOSÉ'S TOMATILLO-PINEAPPLE SALSA

Tomatillos provide the base for the common green table sauces used throughout South and Central America, with each country, even each region, adding its own ingredients to make its version unique. This combination turns up in more than one place, I'm sure, although I saw it most often in the Yucatán. This particular recipe was developed by my talented day chef at the East Coast Grill, José Velasquez.

1 10-ounce can tomatillos or about 12 fresh
  (see Pantry)
½ pineapple, diced small
½ red bell pepper, diced small
½ green bell pepper, diced small
1 medium red onion, diced small
2 tablespoons canned chipotles (see Pantry),
  minced
½ cup chopped cilantro
1 tablespoon minced garlic
¼ cup white vinegar
6 tablespoons lime juice (about 3 limes)
Juice of 2 oranges
Salt and freshly cracked black pepper to taste

1. If using canned tomatillos, purée them in a food processor or blender. If using fresh, chop them fine.

2. To the tomatillos, add the pineapple, red and green bell peppers, and onions.

3. In another bowl, combine the chipotles, cilantro, garlic, vinegar, and lime and orange juice. Stir well.

4. Combine the chipotle mixture with the tomatillo mixture. Stir well and season with salt and pepper to taste. This salsa improves after sitting in the refrigerator for a few hours, and it will keep for 1 week covered and refrigerated.

ABOUT 6 CUPS AS A MAIN COURSE

SERVING SUGGESTIONS: I suggest that you serve this with Sweet Potato Hash Browns with Bacon and Onions (recipe 92).

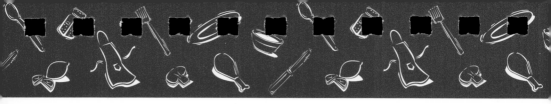

GRILLED POMPANO WITH LIME AND OLIVE OIL

The pompano is an East Coast fish that runs from New England to South America. I know a lot of people in Florida who claim this is the best-eating saltwater fish around. I'm not sure I would say the best, but its flesh combines firmness, sweetness, and tenderness in a way that makes it perfect for grilling. I would never try to impose a lot of spice on this fish, because its strongest characteristic is its subtlety. This fish is a short cooker, and olive oil and lime juice work well with the slight grill flavor that it takes on. If you can get a hold of this fish fresh, buy it and cook it.

4 8-ounce pompano fillets
3 tablespoons vegetable oil
Salt and freshly cracked black pepper to taste
¼ cup extra virgin olive oil
2 limes, halved
2 tablespoons chopped parsley

1. Rub the fillets with vegetable oil and season with salt and pepper to taste.

2. Grill the fillets skin-side up over a medium-hot fire for 3 to 4 minutes. Flip them and cook an additional 2 to 3 minutes, until the fish is opaque all the way through.

3. Remove the fillets from the fire, drizzle them with the olive oil, squeeze a half lime over each, and sprinkle them with the parsley.

SERVES 4 AS A MAIN COURSE

SERVING SUGGESTIONS: Serve this along with Sweet Potato Salad (recipe 93).

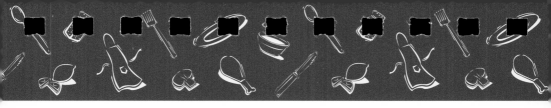

GRILLED YELLOWTAIL WITH WATER CHESTNUT-SCALLION RELISH

◆

MEDIUM

Not to be confused with yellowfin tuna, the yellowtail is a member of the jack family which is present in all tropical and subtropical waters. It spends its days in the Southern Pacific, and the best fishing grounds for it are off the southern California coast. This mild-tasting, large-flaked fish has a firm texture that makes it a natural for grilling. It is definitely one of the top three on my list of fabulous undiscovered food fish. In Mexico, however, it is a very popular fish, and in Japan it is used in sushi known as *hamachi*.

This fish is similar to tuna in that it is appropriate to severely undercook it on the interior while charring it on the exterior. Because of its density, it has a tendency to dry out if overcooked, so check it often and try it a little rare.

The subtly flavored, crunchy Water Chestnut-Scallion Relish with which I accompany the yellowtail is perfect for fish, but it can also be served by itself as a Japanese-style salad. Because of the scallion, this relish won't keep more than a day or two in the refrigerator—best used the day it is made.

4 8- to 10-ounce yellowtail fillets
4 tablespoons vegetable oil
Salt and freshly cracked black pepper to taste

1. Rub the fillets with the vegetable oil, salt and pepper to taste, and grill them over a medium fire, skin-side up, until the top surface has a light golden crust, 5 to 7 minutes.

2. Flip to skin-side down and grill them another 5 to 7 minutes, observing closely and checking often so the fillets don't overcook.

3. Remove the fillets from the grill, and serve accompanied by Water Chestnut-Scallion Relish.

SERVES 4 AS A MAIN COURSE

SERVING SUGGESTIONS: Accompany this with Very Aromatic Tomato-Ginger Jam (recipe 77) or José's Jicama Slaw (recipe 93).

WATER CHESTNUT-SCALLION RELISH

1 cup canned water chestnuts, sliced
1½ cups very thinly sliced scallion (both green and white parts)
1 tablespoon sugar
2 tablespoons sesame seeds, toasted in a single layer in a 350°F oven for 25 minutes
3 tablespoons soy sauce
2 tablespoons sesame oil
3 tablespoons rice wine vinegar

1. In a bowl, combine the sliced water chestnut and scallion. Add the sugar and sesame seeds, and toss well.

2. Add the soy sauce, sesame oil, and vinegar, and toss once again.

3. Serve at once. Will keep covered and refrigerated for only 1 or 2 days.

ABOUT 2 CUPS

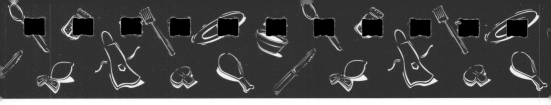

GRILLED TUNA STEAK WITH NECTARINE-RED ONION RELISH

I don't think many cooks will disagree when I say grilling is the best cooking method for tuna—its strong character and distinct flavor allow it to take the grill without being overpowered, and its sturdy texture is extremely durable.

I like to leave the fish a little underdone in the center, as it dries out rapidly if overcooked. The combination here of the sweet and sour taste of the relish against the willful grilled flavor of the tuna is a strong contrast that I find successful.

4 8- to 10-ounce boneless tuna steaks, 1 inch thick
4 tablespoons salad oil
Salt and freshly ground pepper (white is best) to taste

Lightly rub the tuna steaks with oil and season with salt and pepper. Grill the tuna steaks 4 to 5 minutes per side over a medium-hot fire, being careful not to overcook them. Check for doneness by bending a steak gently and peering inside it, looking for a slight translucence in the center. Remove the steaks from the grill and place them on top of the relish.

SERVES 4 AS A MAIN COURSE

SERVING SUGGESTIONS: Serve this with my personal favorite, Your Basic Grilled Corn (recipe 96).

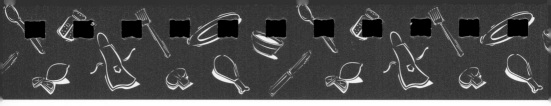

NECTARINE-RED ONION RELISH

I often serve fruit relishes with grilled fish, since the bright, fresh taste of the relishes is excellent against the rather subtle, smoky fish flavors. In tropical climates, fruits like mangoes and papayas are often served in salad form with lime or vinegar. This is a similar treatment, but I've given it an Italian/Mediterranean slant by combining the fruit with red wine vinegar, olive oil, garlic, and basil.

Peaches or plums can be used in place of nectarines in this relish, although the color is not quite as attractive. Whatever fruit you use, it should be firm rather than superripe. Underripe fruit can also be used, but in that case add 1 teaspoon of sugar to the relish to compensate for the lack of sugar in the fruit.

1 red bell pepper, seeded and cut into thin strips
6 ripe but firm nectarines, peeled and cut into 8 slices each
1 medium red onion, sliced into long, thin pieces
1 teaspoon minced garlic
¼ cup julienned fresh basil
¼ cup red wine vinegar
¼ cup fresh orange juice
2 tablespoons lime juice (about 1 lime)
¼ cup virgin olive oil
Salt and freshly cracked black pepper to taste

Combine all the ingredients in a bowl, and toss them gently. It works best if you use a stainless steel bowl much larger than you would think you need for this recipe so you get some real mixing action as you toss. This will be a slightly runny relish, as the solids and liquids mix but do not combine. Keep chilled until ready to serve. This relish will keep, covered and refrigerated, up to 2 weeks.

ABOUT 3 CUPS

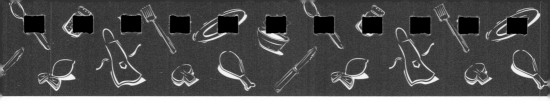

GRILLED SALMON STEAK WITH WATERCRESS, GINGER, AND SESAME

MEDIUM-HIGH

The Indians of the Pacific Northwest were said to revere the salmon as a god. You might think that is going a bit too far, but if you get some superfresh salmon, have your fishmonger cut it into steaks for you, and grill it up, you just might want to join the congregation.

In any case, I agree with Escoffier's precept that salmon should be served as simply as possible. Here a saladlike accompaniment of watercress in a ginger vinaigrette complements the fish's natural flavor. This dish is outstanding served cold the next day, but I would suggest removing the bones from the salmon before refrigerating.

4 12-ounce salmon steaks (1- to 1½-inches thick)
2 tablespoons peanut oil
Salt and freshly cracked black pepper to taste
2 bunches watercress, separated, washed, and dried
½ medium red onion, thinly sliced

FOR THE VINAIGRETTE
2 tablespoons sesame oil
1 teaspoon sugar
2 tablespoons soy sauce
1 tablespoon minced fresh ginger
2 tablespoons rice wine vinegar
2 tablespoons red wine vinegar
¼ cup olive oil
Salt and freshly cracked white pepper to taste

4 tablespoons sesame seeds, toasted in a single layer in 350°F oven for 25 minutes

1. Rub the salmon steaks on both sides with the peanut oil and sprinkle them with salt and pepper to taste. Over a medium-hot fire, grill the steaks 5 to 6 minutes per side. Remove them from the grill.

2. Meanwhile in a salad bowl, combine the watercress and sliced onion. In another bowl, combine all the vinaigrette ingredients and mix well. Pour the vinaigrette onto the watercress-onion mixture and toss lightly.

3. Arrange the dressed watercress on a platter and place the salmon steaks on top. Sprinkle the steaks liberally with the toasted sesame seeds.

SERVES 4 AS A MAIN COURSE

SERVING SUGGESTIONS: Serve it after Grilled Vegetable Antipasto with Braised Garlic Bread (recipe 3).

WHAT IS THE DIFFERENCE BETWEEN A FISH STEAK AND A FISH FILLET?

A steak is cut vertically from the body and includes the backbone, while a fillet is removed horizontally and avoids the bone. Some fish like swordfish are always cut into steaks because of their size and skin texture, while others such as bluefish, snapper, and sole are usually filleted. Yet others, including salmon as well as halibut and striped bass, can be cut in either fashion. In the case of salmon, I prefer the steak because it is slightly less fragile than the fillet and the backbone makes the fish a bit sturdier for grilling. Also, the meat that lies up next to the bone in a steak tastes sweeter to me and seems tenderer than the meat of a fillet.

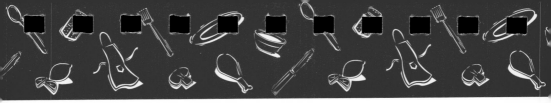

GRILLED SHRIMP WITH DANDELION GREENS AND GINGER

This dish features a nice combination of flavors: the mellow shrimp, the sharpness of the greens, and a little ginger to add a touch of sweetness. Allow your guests to pour the dressing on to their taste.

2 pounds dandelion greens (you may substitute arugula)
1 large red onion
½ red bell pepper, seeded
4 scallions
1 pound 16/20 count (medium-size) shrimp
Salt and freshly cracked black pepper to taste

FOR THE DRESSING
½ cup olive oil
1 tablespoon sesame oil
¼ cup rice wine vinegar
1 tablespoon soy sauce
1 tablespoon minced ginger
1 tablespoon sugar
3 to 6 dashes of Tabasco sauce

4 tablespoons sesame seeds, toasted in a single layer in a 350°F oven for 25 minutes, for garnish

1. Separate, wash, and dry the dandelion greens and put them into a large bowl. Slice the onion, pepper, and scallions very thinly and add them to the greens.

2. Peel and devein the shrimp, thread them on skewers, and season them with salt and pepper to taste.

3. Grill the skewers over a medium fire until the shrimp are completely opaque, about 3 to 4 minutes per side.

4. Meanwhile, whisk the oils, vinegar, soy sauce, ginger, sugar, and Tabasco sauce together in a bowl until homogenous.

5. Add the shrimp to the greens, pour the dresing on, and toss well. Garnish with the toasted sesame seeds.

SERVING SUGGESTIONS: Serve this with Grilled Basque Wings (recipe 12).

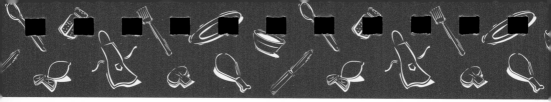

GRILLED SWORDFISH STEAKS WITH YUCATÁN ORANGE-HERB PASTE

◆

MEDIUM

In this preparation it is important to cut the swordfish steaks thinly so the paste doesn't burn before the fish is cooked. Pastes like the one used here are common in tropical countries, since they lend intensity and complexity to simple grilled foods. This approach is similar to the Cajun "blackening" technique.

FOR THE PASTE
1 teaspoon minced garlic
1 teaspoon ground cumin
1 teaspoon chili powder
2 tablespoons chopped fresh oregano
2 tablespoons chopped cilantro
6 tablespoons orange juice combined with 2 tablespoons lime juice
4 dashes of Tabasco sauce
2 tablespoons extra virgin olive oil

4 10-ounce swordfish steaks, cut ½- to 1-inch thick
Vegetable oil for brushing

1. Make the paste: In a food processor or blender, combine all the ingredients, purée, and set aside.

2. Brush the swordfish steaks with vegetable oil. Over a medium fire, grill the swordfish steaks, 4 to 5 minutes per side, or until they are almost completely opaque.

3. Brush 3 quarters of the paste onto both sides of the swordfish steaks and cook an additional 1 minute per side.

4. Remove the swordfish steaks from the grill, brush on the remaining paste, and serve.

SERVES 4 AS A MAIN COURSE

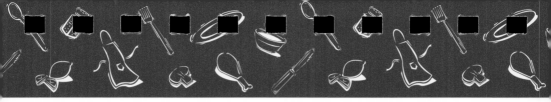

GRILLED STEAMED LITTLENECKS JOHNSON

◆

I got this recipe from my friend Steve Johnson, who owns a catering company. He found that this simple preparation made a nice display on the grill while he was cooking other dishes, and I recommend that you try it. Just set the butter-wine pan on the cool side of the grill and whip the clams in there as they open up. Eat some yourself while you cook, and when folks wander over to admire your incredible creativity at the grill, offer 'em a clam.

If you want to make the presentation slightly more elegant (or if you just don't like serving clams in their shells), you can remove the shells and serve the clams as they are or over pasta.

½ pound unsalted butter
½ cup white wine
36 littleneck clams
2 lemons, cut in half
2 tablespoons chopped parsley
Salt and freshly cracked pepper to taste (white is best if you have it)

1. Combine the butter and wine in a shallow baking pan that can hold all of the clams and withstand low heat on your grill.

2. Wash the clams well to remove sand and excess dirt.

3. Approach the grill: You should have your tongs, your pan containing the butter and wine, a serving platter, and another large platter containing the clams, lemons, parsley, and salt and pepper. Some particular attention should be paid to the fire for this preparation. You want to have

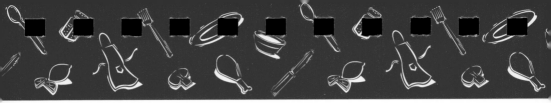

half of your fire medium-high heat, and the other half medium-low.

4. Place the pan with the butter and wine in it on the low-heat side of the grill, and place the clams on the rack on the high-heat side.

5. The clams will open when cooked. This should take about 8 to 11 minutes, depending on your fire.

6. As the clams open, place them in the butter-wine mixture. When all the clams have opened, place them on a serving platter, squeeze the lemon halves over them, and sprinkle them with parsley and salt and pepper to taste.

SERVES 4 AS A LIGHT MAIN COURSE

SERVING SUGGESTIONS: Serve this as a light main course. It pairs well with Grilled Shrimp Pasta with Sun-Dried Tomatoes and Basil (recipe 37) or Grilled Chicken Breast with Fresh Herbs and Lemon (recipe 57) for a more hearty meal. For a very esoteric dinner, serve it followed by Grilled Venison Loin with Bourbon Peaches (recipe 61).

GRILLED SEA SCALLOPS WITH COCONUT-CHILE SAUCE

◆

A little Indonesian treatment here. I like the combination of the smooth texture of the scallops and the velvety flavor of the coconut milk, with some red chile pepper flakes added so that no one falls asleep. The thin consistency of the sauce belies its intensity. This goes well with plain steamed white rice. Use chopped scallions and toasted sesame seeds for garnish if you want to break out the china for this one.

½ cup coconut milk (see Pantry)
4 tablespoons lime juice (about 2 limes)
1 teaspoon fresh minced ginger
1 teaspoon red pepper flakes
2 tablespoons chopped cilantro
1½ pounds large sea scallops
Salt and freshly cracked black pepper to taste

1. Make the sauce in a bowl, combine the coconut milk, lime juice, and ginger, and mix well.

2. Add the pepper flakes and cilantro, and mix well. Set aside. This will be a thin, very light, milky sauce.

3. Put the scallops in boiling water to cover for 1 minute (otherwise they stick to the grill). Drain them, thread them on skewers, and season them with salt and pepper to taste.

4. On a hot fire, cook the scallops until light brown, 2 to 3 minutes per side.

5. Remove the scallops from the skewers, pour the sauce over them, and serve with a small amount of white rice.

SERVES 4 AS A MAIN COURSE

SERVING SUGGESTIONS: Serve this with East Coast Grill Corn Bread (recipe 99).

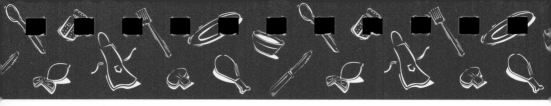

GRILLED SAUSAGE AND SCALLOPS WITH PEPPERS, LEMON, BASIL, AND GARLIC

◆

MEDIUM

Scallops are so delicate they stick to the grill unless you blanch them first. Sausages also have to be precooked, or they burn on the grill before they are cooked. Try this dish with heavily garlicked bread.

1½ pounds fresh sea scallops
4 freshly ground sausage links (3 to 4 ounces each)
1 large yellow onion, cut into cubes
1 large red bell pepper, seeded and cut into about 12 large squares
1 large green bell pepper, seeded and cut into about 12 large squares
Salt and freshly cracked black pepper to taste
4 tablespoons chopped fresh basil
1 teaspoon minced garlic
2 tablespoons extra virgin olive oil
8 tablespoons lemon juice (about 2 lemons)
2 tablespoons balsamic vinegar

1. Blanch the scallops in boiling salted water for 1 minute. Drain and allow to cool.

2. Cook the sausage in boiling water until completely cooked, approximately 5 minutes. Drain and allow to cool.

3. Thread the scallops, sausages, and vegetables on skewers and season with salt and pepper to taste.

4. Cook the skewers over a medium fire until all the ingredients have attained some brown crusting, about 3 to 4 minutes per side.

5. Slide the scallops, sausages, and vegetables off the skewers into a large bowl. Add the basil, garlic, oil, lemon juice, and balsamic vinegar. Shake the bowl until everything is well mixed and serve.

SERVES 4 AS A MAIN COURSE

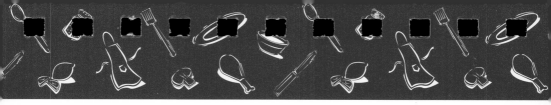

CARIBBEAN-STYLE GRILLED SEAFOOD SOUP

Even though this soup is served hot, it is an excellent choice for a hot summer day because it is also spicy. This follows a precept commonly accepted in tropical cultures, that eating hot foods will bring your body temperature down and make you feel cooler. (My travels in tropical areas bear this out, and as a matter of fact, this isn't limited to tropical cultures. A friend of mine who grew up in Iowa—decidedly untropical—tells how his grandfather always used to drink hot coffee when baling hay in the broiling Midwest sun, since it gave him more relief from the heat than the cold lemonade that others drank.)

Unlike most soups of this type, in which the fish is actually cooked in the broth, here the seafood is grilled and then added to the broth at the very end. This prevents overcooking and also keeps the individual flavors of the different seafoods strong and distinct. The broth serves as a background, but it is also flavorful and spicy in its own right.

This recipe is easily doubled and makes a fantastic meal with salad and bread. It is one of my personal favorites.

10 16/20 count (medium-size) shrimp, peeled and deveined
12 medium sea scallops
1 10-ounce mackerel or kingfish fillet
1 8- to 10-ounce spiny lobster tail, shelled (available frozen in supermarkets)
3 tablespoons vegetable oil
2 large yellow onions, diced small
3 stalks celery, diced small
2 tablespoons minced garlic
1 cup white wine
1½ quarts bottled clam juice
½ teaspoon ground cumin
¼ teaspoon allspice

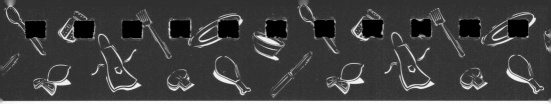

2 large sweet potatoes, cut into large cubes
½ pound fresh okra, thickly sliced
2 fresh tomatoes, cut into large chunks
Salt and freshly cracked pepper to taste (white
    is best if you have it)
4 tablespoons lime juice (about 2 limes)
2 tablespoons minced fresh green or red chile
    peppers of your choice
3 tablespoons chopped cilantro

1. Over a hot fire, grill each kind of seafood separately. The shrimp will take approximately 3 to 4 minutes per side, the scallops 3 minutes per side, the kingfish 5 minutes per side, and the lobster 4 minutes per side. As each is done, remove it from the grill, and set aside. (Note: You are looking for the seafood to get some color on its surface: Don't worry too much about cooking it completely, since it will finish in the broth.)

2. In a large saucepan or soup pot, heat the oil until very hot but not smoking. Sauté the onion and celery in the hot oil until clear, about 5 minutes. Add the garlic, and sauté an additional minute.

3. Add the wine, clam juice, cumin, and allspice to the pot, and bring to a simmer.

4. Add the sweet potato, okra, and tomato, and continue to simmer for 30 minutes.

5. At this point, add any of the seafood that is not completely cooked, and simmer for 4 more minutes.

6. Just before serving, add the remainder of the seafood, and simmer for 1 minute, just to warm it through. Remove the pot from the heat and add salt and pepper to taste. Just before serving, toss in the lime juice, chile peppers, and cilantro, and stir briefly.

SERVES 6 AS A MAIN COURSE

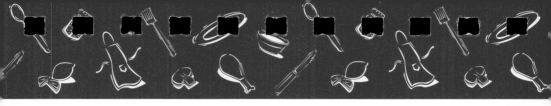

GRILLED SCALLOPS WITH ROCOTILLO-MANGO RELISH

This Caribbean-inspired dish features the rocotillo pepper. The sharp spiciness (*not* heat) of the pepper combines easily with the mellow sweetness of the mango, creating a strong but not overpowering accompaniment for the creamy taste of the scallops.

1 cup fresh green or red rocotillo chile peppers (you may substitute your favorite chile peppers)
1 small red onion
1 green bell pepper, seeded
1 red bell pepper, seeded
2 ripe mangoes, cleaned
Juice of 3 oranges
½ cup pineapple juice
8 tablespoons lime juice (about 4 limes)
¼ cup chopped cilantro
2 pounds sea scallops
Salt and freshly cracked black pepper to taste

1. Dice the rocotillos, onion, bell peppers, and mangoes.

2. In a large mixing bowl, combine the diced ingredients with all the remaining ingredients except the scallops, and mix well. Season with salt and pepper to taste.

3. Blanch the scallops in boiling water for 1 minute (otherwise they stick to the grill). Drain and pat them dry and sprinkle them with salt and pepper to taste.

4. Thread the scallops on skewers and grill them over a medium-hot fire until they are golden brown outside and opaque throughout, about 2 to 3 minutes per side.

5. Make a bed of the relish on each plate and place the scallops on top.

SERVES 8 AS AN APPETIZER OR 4 AS A MAIN COURSE

SMALL THINGS TO COOK IN THE COALS

◆

There are any number of small treats you can make for yourself as long as you are grilling anyway. Just rub them with salt and freshly cracked black pepper to taste, wrap them in foil with the accompanying items, and throw them in the coals to cook. The proportions will depend upon your individual taste.

Zucchinis, cut into 1-inch slices, with garlic, thyme, and olive oil

Halved red onions with rosemary and balsamic vinegar

Small red potatoes with butter and garlic

Mushrooms with butter, sherry, and basil

Sweet potatoes, cut into 1-inch slices, with brown sugar and butter

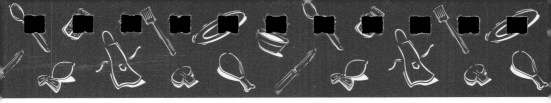

GRILLED RUM-SOAKED SHRIMP WITH MANGO-LIME RELISH

◆

I'm not sure exactly why, but I always get a big kick out of grilling shrimp. I leave the skins on the shrimp to protect the meat from burning while grilling. Because of this, you'll want to pay some attention to the size of the shrimp you use, since the bigger the shrimp the easier they are to peel.

The slight rum flavor in the shrimp and the mango-lime relish reproduce the island/beach inspiration of this dish. It's a fun dish that requires your guests to participate by peeling their own food.

32 16/20 count (medium-size) shrimp (about 2 pounds)
8 tablespoons lime juice (about 4 limes)
1½ cups canned pineapple juice
½ cup dark rum
2 tablespoons finely chopped cilantro
1 teaspoon chopped garlic
Salt and freshly cracked black pepper to taste

1. Peel the shrimp and make a ¼-inch-deep incision on the top of each one (the side without the feet) from tail to head. Under cold running water, open the incision and wash away any brownish-black waste matter.

2. In a large stainless steel bowl, combine the lime juice, pineapple juice, rum, cilantro, garlic, and salt and pepper to taste. Add the shrimp. Cover and refrigerate and allow the shrimp to soak in the marinade for 2 to 4 hours—no longer, or they will start to cook in the lime juice. Remove the shrimp from the marinade and discard it.

3. Run a skewer through each shrimp so it is skewered in two places: Put the skewer through the tail area, then bend the shrimp over and put the skewer through the thick section in the upper body area. You should be able to fit 4 shrimp on a 6" skewer, 8 on a 10" skewer. (If you are using wooden

skewers, be careful not to leave any gaps between the shrimp, or the skewer will burn through and the fire will get the shrimp.)

4. Place the skewered shrimp on the grill over medium-high heat. Grill about 3 to 4 minutes on each side, until the shells turn bright red. It's easy to check to see if they are done by probing the incision you made in Step 1. The meat should be an even opaque white.

5. Remove the shrimp from the grill and serve them on a bed of Mango-Lime Relish, either skewered or unskewered as you prefer.

SERVES 4 AS A MAIN COURSE OR 8 AS AN APPETIZER

SERVING SUGGESTIONS: As a first course, I follow it with a big, hearty meat course such as Grilled Lamb Steaks with Rosemary, Garlic, and Red Wine (recipe 41) or Simple Grilled Whole Beef Tenderloin (recipe 48). As a main course, accompany it with West Indies Breadfruit Salad (recipe 91).

MANGO-LIME RELISH

3 ripe mangoes
1 small red bell pepper, seeded
1 small green bell pepper, seeded
1 small red onion
1 cup canned pineapple juice
4 tablespoons lime juice (about 2 limes)
1 teaspoon chopped garlic
15 to 20 whole cilantro leaves
4 tablespoons red wine vinegar
1 tablespoon curry powder
Salt and freshly cracked black pepper to taste

1. Peel the mangoes and, using a sharp knife, slice the fruit away from the central pit.

2. Dice the mango fruit, red pepper, green pepper, and onion.

3. Combine all the remaining ingredients in a bowl. Mix lightly, then add the diced mango, pepper, and onion, and mix once again. This texture will keep 3 days, covered, in the refrigerator.

ABOUT 2½ CUPS

GRILLED SHRIMP PASTA WITH SUN-DRIED TOMATOES AND BASIL

MEDIUM

I love grilled shrimp and will eat them any way I can get them. Here I use them with pasta and basil for a refreshing light dinner entrée for a hot summer evening.

2 pounds 16/20 count (medium-size) shrimp
Salt and freshly cracked black pepper to taste
1 pound fettuccine
12 sun-dried tomatoes, cut into thin strips (see Pantry)
¼ cup fresh black olives, halved and pitted
1 tablespoon minced garlic
1 tablespoon capers
½ cup chopped fresh basil
¼ cup pine nuts, toasted
2 tablespoons unsalted butter, cut into eighths
4 tablespoons lemon juice (about 1 lemon)
Lemon wedges for garnish
Basil leaves for garnish
½ cup grated Romano cheese

1. Peel and devein the shrimp and remove their tails.

2. Thread the shrimp on skewers, season with salt and pepper to taste, and grill them 3 to 4 minutes per side over medium heat.

3. Cook the fettuccine in 4 quarts of boiling salted water until al dente, 8 to 10 minutes for dried, 3 to 4 for fresh. Drain and put it into a large bowl.

4. Add the tomatoes, olives, garlic, capers, basil, pine nuts, and butter, and toss well. Season with salt and pepper to taste, then stir in the lemon juice.

5. Add the shrimp to the bowl, garnish with the lemon wedges and basil leaves, and serve with grated Romano in a separate bowl.

SERVES 4 AS A MAIN COURSE

GRILLED SHRIMP WITH GREENS, BACON, AND SWEET POTATO

MEDIUM

I've said it once and I'll say it again— grilled shrimp make me happy. Their small size means they don't stay on the grill long enough to acquire a char that overcomes the delicate flavor, and their firm texture lets them remain juicy through the quick searing.

16 16/20 count (medium-size) shrimp (about 1 pound)
Salt and freshly cracked black pepper to taste
½ pound slab bacon, medium-diced
1 cup cooked sweet potatoes (about ½ pound), diced small
1 pound chicory, cleaned, washed, and dried
½ pound mixed greens (mustard, beet, turnip, dandelion, etc.), cleaned, washed, and dried
¼ cup balsamic vinegar
Pinch of sugar

1. Peel and devein the shrimp, but leave the tails on. Thread them on skewers, season with salt and pepper to taste, and grill them over a medium fire, 3 to 4 minutes per side. Remove and set them aside.

2. Sauté the bacon over medium heat until crisp, about 5 minutes, and remove it from pan. Do not pour off the bacon fat. Instead, add the sweet potatoes, and cook for 2 minutes. Then add the chicory and greens and turn furiously, just until the leaves are well covered with the bacon fat.

3. Remove the greens mixture from the heat, add the vinegar, sugar, and salt and pepper to taste, and toss. Place a portion on individual plates and put a skewer of shrimp on each.

SERVES 4 AS AN APPETIZER OR 2 AS A MAIN COURSE

SERVING SUGGESTIONS: Serve this in front of Grilled Butterflied Leg o' Lamb (recipe 43).

SOY-MARINATED SCALLOPS WITH GRILLED SHIITAKES

Generally speaking, small bay scallops are prized over the larger sea scallops. For this dish, however, I prefer sea scallops; their size allows them to char on the outside before they become overcooked on the inside. When buying them, try to choose scallops of uniform size; the fishmonger might not be too happy about matching sizes, but that will usually be offset by his or her joy at unloading those giant scallops.

This dish is straightforward: The strong soy and ginger taste of the marinade goes well with the grilled scallops. I don't use a sauce here because you want the marinade to be present and the scallop taste to stand out. Rounding out the Japanese motif, I grill some shiitake mushrooms. Here again, choose the monster mushrooms. When grilled, the shiitakes react almost like meat, with the outside becoming crisp and the inside remaining tender and moist.

2 pounds sea scallops
8 tablespoons soy sauce
4 tablespoons rice wine vinegar
1 tablespoon grated ginger
1 tablespoon sesame oil
1 teaspoon white pepper
1 teaspoon sugar
4 monster or 8 medium shiitakes
2 tablespoons vegetable oil
Salt and freshly cracked black pepper to taste
Freshly cracked pepper to taste (white is best if you have it)
2 tablespoons sesame seeds, toasted in a single layer in a 350°F oven for 25 minutes

1. Rinse the scallops thoroughly and set aside.

2. In a stainless steel bowl, combine the soy sauce, vinegar, ginger, sesame oil, white pepper, and sugar, and mix well.

3. Put the scallops in the marinade

mixture, cover them, and place in the refrigerator for 4 to 6 hours, turning once or twice. (No longer, or the marinade will dominate the scallop flavor.)

4. If the shiitakes are dirty, clean them by wiping them gently with a cloth or paper towel. Rub them with the vegetable oil, and season them with salt and pepper to taste.

5. Remove the scallops from the marinade and drain them. Season them with pepper to taste (no salt is needed on the scallops because of the saltiness of the marinade).

6. Place the scallops individually over a medium-high gas grill or medium-hot fire. If the scallops are too small or the spaces on the grill too large to allow you to do this, you will need to skewer them.

7. Cook the scallops, rolling them around a bit, 3 to 5 minutes, until firm. (To be sure, take one off and cut it open.)

8. At the same time you cook the scallops, if there is room on the grill, put the shiitakes on, and grill them about 3 to 5 minutes. When they have darkened slightly

and have crisp exteriors, remove them from the grill and serve them with the scallops, garnished with the toasted sesame seeds.

SERVES 4 AS A MAIN COURSE

SERVING SUGGESTIONS: Serve this along with José's Jicama Slaw (recipe 89), a simple buttered pasta, and lightly grilled red bell peppers.

GRILL-SEARED SUSHI-QUALITY TUNA WITH SOY, WASABI, AND PICKLED GINGER

◆

While this dish appears to be simple, it possesses an Eastern complexity within its seeming simplicity. It is one of the most popular dishes in the East Coast Grill, and is representative of some of the principles essential to my style of food.

The inspiration for this particular method of preparation comes from my dad, who insisted on grilling steaks so they were burned on the outside and raw on the inside. My sister and I would always tell him that it was both too burned and too raw, but he would say that was the way meat should be cooked. He refused to cook steaks any other way, so we eventually got to like them. Tuna cooked by this method has a texture very similar to rare steak, and much like my sister and me, many of our customers find that they like this prepara-

tion despite their initial skepticism. We are always pleased to see how many people try it and how many tunas don't make the return trip to the grill. So even if you're not sure about this method, try it! If you don't like it, just toss it back on the grill.

When I serve this, I put the soy in a little dish along with the wasabi on an orange wedge, and serve the ginger on the side. Japanese like to mix the wasabi together with the soy, and they use the ginger to clean the tastebuds.

4 8-ounce tuna steaks (3 inches thick)
4 tablespoons sesame oil
Salt and freshly ground pepper to taste (white is best if you have it)
¾ cup pickled ginger (gari) (see Pantry)

*6 tablespoons wasabi powder (see Pantry) mixed
with water to the consistency of wet sand*
12 tablespoons soy sauce

1. Brush the tuna steaks lightly with the sesame oil and season with salt and pepper to taste.

2. Over high heat, place the steaks on the grill and cook 4 to 5 minutes on the top and bottom sides, or until a dark brown crispy skin has been formed.

3. Now cook the steaks for 2 to 3 minutes on each edge, trying to achieve the same dark brown crispy effect.

4. Remove the steaks from the grill, and serve with gari, wasabi, and soy sauce.

SERVES 4 AS A MAIN COURSE

SERVING SUGGESTIONS: The tuna is the star of the main course, so don't serve anything to compete with it. Use simple side dishes like Grilled Eggplant with Olive Oil, Parsley, and Capers (recipe 94), and plain white rice.

The "sushi-quality" tuna used here is somewhat difficult to find because what you are looking for is absolute freshness. To test for this, ask your fishmonger if you can smell the tuna. If it smells like fish, don't even consider using it here. This does not mean that the fish is not fine to eat when cooked, but when eating fish rare to raw, the taste of the fish itself comes through much more clearly.

The tuna (for example, an 8-ounce steak) has to be cut very thick, about 3 inches, so it resembles a filet mignon. To get the proper cut, it is essential to enlist the aid of your fishmonger. The thick cut ensures that, although the fish is cooked very hard over very high heat so it is seared/charred on the outside, it will remain raw on the inside.

BIRDS AND
THINGS WITH
HOOVES

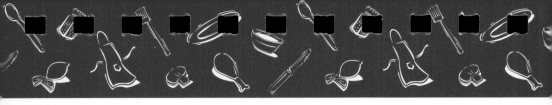

GRILLED LAMB STEAKS WITH ROSEMARY, GARLIC, AND RED WINE

As a child traveling in Greece with my family, I had the best lamb I ever tasted. On the way to the Oracle at Delphi, my sister and I insisted that we stop at every roadside bar and sample the lamb skewers, which were rubbed with rosemary and garlic.

I think that cutting a leg of lamb into steaks works well because the leg has enough muscle tissue to give it a very nice flavor, but not so much that it is tough.

2 tablespoons minced garlic
2 tablespoons fresh rosemary
6-pound leg of lamb, cut into 6 steaks (have
    your butcher do this for you), bone in
½ cup dry red wine
1 cup olive oil
Salt and freshly cracked black pepper to taste

1. Make a paste of the garlic and rosemary and rub it into the steaks *con mucho gusto*.

2. Put the steaks into a shallow dish, add the wine and olive oil, and let the steaks wallow around in the mixture, covered, for about 2 hours.

3. Remove the steaks, season them with salt and pepper to taste, and hit the grill. Grill them over a medium-high fire, 6 to 8 minutes per side for medium rare. Serve with lemon wedges and pita.

SERVES 6 AS A MAIN COURSE

SERVING SUGGESTIONS: This dish is great served with grilled spring onions and pita.

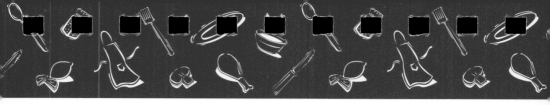

SWEET MILK-MARINATED GRILLED LAMB WITH SWEET AND HOT APRICOT CONDIMENT

MEDIUM-HIGH

Here's a good example of the kind of grilling festivities that go on in other countries. In South Africa, there is a strong tradition of backyard grilling, which they call "braa-ing." The most popular types of dishes for braa-ing are called *sos saties*, a term derived from two Malay words meaning "spiced sauce" and "skewered meat." *Sos saties* are like barbecue in the United States in that everybody has his or her own particular recipe, which of course is the only authentic one.

This dish, in which the process of marinating meat in milk again shows the strong East Indian/Indonesian influence, is a variation of a classic *sos saties*. The sweet and hot apricot condiment is my version of a South African "sambal," a type of sweet, hot, aromatic condiment traditionally served with curries.

2½ pounds lamb, cut into 1-inch cubes

FOR THE MARINADE
1 cup milk
1 cup vinegar
2 tablespoons curry powder
2 tablespoons brown sugar
1 tablespoon chili powder
2 tablespoons minced garlic
1 teaspoon turmeric
1 teaspoon red pepper flakes
1 teaspoon black pepper
1 teaspoon coriander seed
Salt and freshly cracked pepper to taste

1. Put the cubed lamb into a large shallow dish.

2. Combine all the marinade ingredients, mix well, and pour over the lamb.

3. Cover the dish and let the lamb sit

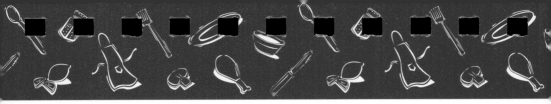

in the marinade for approximately 24 hours, refrigerated, stirring occasionally.

4. Remove the lamb from the marinade, pat it dry, and season it with salt and pepper to taste. Thread the cubes on skewers. (Discard marinade.)

5. Over a medium-hot fire, grill the lamb skewers approximately 5 to 7 minutes per side. The meat should be juicy and pink inside. After removing the lamb from the grill, allow it to sit 3 to 5 minutes before serving it, accompanied by Sweet and Hot Apricot Condiment.

SERVES 4 AS A MAIN COURSE OR 8 AS AN APPETIZER

SERVING SUGGESTIONS: Serve this with Sweet Potato Salad (recipe 93) or Grilled Steamed Littlenecks Johnson (recipe 31).

SWEET AND HOT APRICOT CONDIMENT

2 large yellow onions, thickly sliced
4 tablespoons peanut oil
½ cup dried apricots
¼ cup raisins
½ cup grated fresh coconut (you may substitute ¼ cup dried unsweetened coconut)
¼ cup white vinegar
¼ cup apricot jelly
3 tablespoons chopped fresh hot chile pepper
Salt and freshly cracked black pepper to taste
4 tablespoons lemon juice (about 1 lemon)

1. Sauté the onion in peanut oil over medium-high heat until golden, 5 to 7 minutes.

2. Add the apricots, raisins, and coconut to the sauté pan, and continue to cook for 2 minutes.

3. Add the vinegar and jelly and cook for 1 minute.

4. Add the hot chile pepper and salt and pepper to taste and remove from the heat.

5. Just before serving, shoot the lemon juice into the mixture. This will keep, covered, and refrigerated, for about 2 weeks.

ABOUT 2 CUPS

GRILLED BUTTERFLIED
LEG O' LAMB

Lamb is an outstanding meat for grilling. A butterflied leg o' lamb is easy to find, but if the leg you get is boned and not butterflied, it is easy to do it yourself. Simply make one cut almost completely through the lamb to lay it open, then put it on a counter and cover it with plastic wrap. Next take a mallet or heavy frying pan and whack it a couple of times, keeping in mind that your object is to flatten the meat to make the cooking time quicker (you are looking for a thickness of about 2 to 3 inches).

1 4- to 5-pound boneless, butterflied leg
   o' lamb
3 tablespoons minced garlic
3 tablespoons chopped fresh basil
3 tablespoons chopped fresh rosemary
3 tablespoons chopped fresh thyme
Salt and freshly cracked black pepper to taste

1. Make a paste of the garlic and seasonings by mashing them together thoroughly in a mortar and pestle—or use a heavy wooden spoon and a bowl. Rub this paste into the lamb and allow it to sit at room temperature for 1 hour.

2. Build a fire in one side of your covered grill. Over high heat, sear both sides of the lamb directly over the coals until well-browned, about 4 to 5 minutes per side.

3. Move the lamb to the half of the grill with no coals, cover, and cook for 15 to 20 minutes. At the 10-minute mark, check the meat by nicking a side. Remove the lamb from the grill when it is done to your liking, and allow it to rest 5 to 10 minutes before slicing it into ½-inch slices and serving.

SERVES 6 TO 8 AS A MAIN COURSE

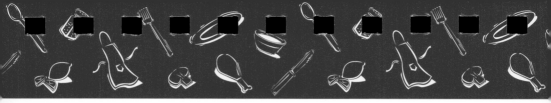

GRILLED COUNTRY HAM
AND APPLESAUCE

A standard item in my grandma's reper-toire—I grill the ham here, which is something Grandma never did, and add a little maple syrup glaze.

FOR THE APPLESAUCE (ABOUT 5 CUPS)
10 Baldwin or McIntosh apples, peeled, cored, and quartered
¼ cup maple syrup
⅓ cup sugar
½ cup orange juice
½ teaspoon cinnamon
⅛ teaspoon nutmeg
⅛ teaspoon allspice

FOR THE HAM
3-pound semiboneless Jones or other cured ham
Salt and freshly cracked black pepper to taste
4 tablespoons maple syrup

1. Make the applesauce: Put the apple quar-ters, maple syrup, sugar, orange juice, and spices into a stockpot. Bring to a simmer, reduce the heat, and simmer slowly for 30 to 45 minutes, stirring occasionally. The apple quarters should be quite soft.

2. Using a food processor, blender, or potato masher, purée or mash the apple-sauce, then put it through a strainer. Allow it to cool to room temperature before serving. It will keep, covered and refrigerat-ed, for 3 to 5 days.

3. Slice the ham into ¼-inch-thick slices and season on both sides with salt and pepper to taste.

4. Over a medium fire, grill the ham on one side for 4 to 5 minutes, until well-seared. During the last minute of cooking, brush it with maple syrup.

SERVES 8 AS A MAIN COURSE

GRILLED VEAL CHOP WITH ARTICHOKE HEARTS, SUN-DRIED TOMATOES, AND PINE NUTS

◆

MEDIUM-LOW

I usually stay away from veal when grilling for two reasons: First, the subtle flavor and tenderness that you pay for when you buy veal is covered up by the grilling process; and second, I think pork is more flavorful and makes a fine substitute in most veal recipes. The veal chop is the sole exception. This is not a dainty cut, and because of its mass it can stand up to grilling quite well. The large bone in the chop provides the necessary durability, protecting the meat and keeping it tender.

In other words, this is a delicate meat in the form of a hearty cut, and therefore suitable for a strong preparation. We get back to featuring the subtlety by serving it with a mild relish of fresh artichoke hearts and sun-dried tomatoes.

4 fresh artichokes
4 tablespoons olive oil
8 tablespoons lemon juice (about 2 lemons)
8 sun-dried tomatoes, finely julienned (see Pantry)
¼ cup Kalamata black olives, halved and pitted
¼ cup fresh basil, julienned
4 tablespoons pine nuts, toasted
4 veal chops (12 to 14 ounces each, at least 1 inch thick)

1. Prepare the artichoke hearts: Remove the outside leaves from the artichokes, and cut off the top two thirds of the artichokes. Remove the chokes and trim around the outside, leaving only the hearts. Cook the hearts in boiling salted water to

cover until tender, 8 to 10 minutes. Remove from the heat, drain, and cool. When cool, slice each heart into 4 slices.

2. In a small bowl, combine the olive oil with the lemon juice. Place the artichoke hearts in the bowl and toss gently to cover with the oil-juice mixture. Add the sun-dried tomatoes, olives, basil, and pine nuts, and mix well. Set aside.

3. You want a medium-low fire for the chops, since searing is not as important with white veal meat as it is with red meat. Over this fire, cook the chops for 8 to 10 minutes per side. Check for doneness by nicking one of the chops and peeking at the interior. It should be slightly pink for medium, which is how I like to cook veal.

4. Remove the veal from the grill and allow it to repose for 5 minutes. Serve each chop topped with a couple of tablespoons of relish.

SERVES 4 AS A MAIN COURSE

SERVING SUGGESTIONS: Serve this with Grilled Eggplant with Olive Oil, Parsley, and Capers (recipe 90), or preceded by Steamed Clams with Lemongrass and Chiles de Árbol (recipe 5) as an appetizer.

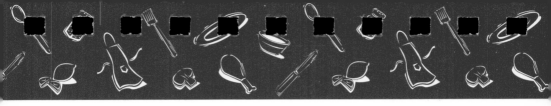

GRILLED LIME-MARINATED FLANK STEAK WITH CHIPOTLE-HONEY SAUCE

The flank is not the tenderest cut of beef, but it may be the most flavorful. To make it tenderer, I marinate it and slice it against the grain very thin on the bias after cooking it. So what you start with is very thin steak, and what you end up with is large thin slices of char-flavored meat that resembles roast beef. The acid in the lime marinade is very complementary to the char flavor of the meat. Marinate it anywhere from 4 to 6 hours; any longer than that and the lime juice will actually cook the steak, leaving you with gray meat.

Make sure your grill is really hot. Because this thin cut of meat takes very little time to cook, you need that intense heat to give it the color you want.

The sauce is a sweet/hot combination that features chipotles, which are dried smoked jalapeño chile peppers with a very distinctive flavor. Adjust the heat to the level you want, using the chipotle as your fuel.

FOR THE MARINADE
1 canned chipotle, chopped (see Pantry)
2 garlic cloves, minced
1 tablespoon chopped cilantro
4 tablespoons vegetable oil
10 tablespoons lime juice (about 5 limes)

FOR THE SAUCE
¼ cup honey
2 tablespoons peanut oil
3 to 5 (depends on how hot you want this)
   canned chipotles
2 tablespoons balsamic vinegar
2 tablespoons brown mustard
8 tablespoons lime juice (about 4 limes)

2 garlic cloves
1 teaspoon ground cumin
2 tablespoons chopped cilantro
1 teaspoon salt
Salt and freshly cracked black pepper to taste

1. Place the steak in a large dish or baking pan. Mix all the marinade ingredients together, then pour the marinade over the steak. Cover the steak and let it marinate in the refrigerator for 4 to 6 hours, turning occasionally.

2. Make the sauce: Combine the honey, peanut oil, chipotles, vinegar, mustard, lime juice, garlic, and cumin, and purée in a blender or food processor. Stir in the chopped cilantro and add the salt and pepper to taste.

3. Salt and pepper the steak to taste. Over very high heat, grill the steak for 5 to 7 minutes on each side (for medium rare).

4. Remove the steak from the grill and let it rest for 3 to 5 minutes so the juices that were drawn to the center by cooking redistribute for even color. Then, using a very sharp knife, slice the steak as thin as you can, against the grain and on a very sharp angle.

5. Serve the steak, which should be very juicy, either plain or on top of sliced French bread, and accompany each serving with several tablespoons of the sauce.

SERVES 4 AS A MAIN COURSE

SERVING SUGGESTIONS: Black Bean Salad (recipe 95) and fresh tortillas combine well with this dish for a full dinner.

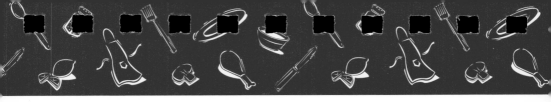

GRILLED TOP ROUND, CUBAN STYLE, WITH PLÁTANOS FRITOS

HIGH

This dish provides an interesting combination of classic Caribbean ingredients with an Asian twist. I use round steak here, which can often be found under the obsequious name of London broil. The key to the taste of the meat in this dish is complete and total searing, which develops a heavy crust with a distinctive grilled flavor that stands up to the spicy preparation.

The fried plantains are a staple of Caribbean and Central American cuisine, and this is the standard preparation, which calls for them to be fried once, smashed, and then fried again. Make sure you use green plantains, because in this state they are more like a potato than a banana, which they resemble when they are ripe.

1 2½-pound top round steak, about 1½ inches thick
Salt and freshly cracked black pepper to taste
1 large red onion
1 red bell pepper, seeded
1 green bell pepper, seeded
10 radishes
¼ cup virgin olive oil
1 tablespoon Tabasco sauce
1 tablespoon minced garlic
2 tablespoons finely chopped parsley
2 tablespoons finely chopped cilantro
1 tablespoon ground cumin
1 tablespoon chili powder
6 tablespoons lime juice (about 3 limes)

1. Season the meat with salt and pepper all over and grill it over a hot fire. You want to grill it until it is dark brown and very crusty—the crustiness is the key to the taste of this preparation. The inside should

be rare/medium rare, which should take 4 to 6 minutes per side.

2. Remove the meat from the grill and let it stand about 5 minutes.

3. Cut the meat into cubes about the size of dice. (The kind that roll, not the kind you hang from your rearview mirror.)

4. Put the diced meat into a large mixing bowl. Dice the red onion and red and green bell peppers, slice the radishes very thin, and mix well with the meat.

5. Add all the remaining ingredients except the lime juice and toss well.

6. Seconds before serving, add the lime juice and toss one more time. Serve with Plátanos Fritos and rice and beans.

SERVES 4 AS A MAIN COURSE

SERVING SUGGESTIONS: This is a fairly loud dish, and I would recommend serving it with Your Basic Black Beans (recipe 95) or plain boiled rice.

PLÁTANOS FRITOS

2 green plantains
2 cups vegetable oil
Salt and freshly cracked black pepper to taste

1. Peel the plantains and cut them into 2-inch rounds.

2. In a small saucepot, heat the oil until very hot but not smoking.

3. Drop the plantain rounds into the oil three at a time and cook them until well browned, about 2 to 3 minutes. Remove them from the oil and drain them on a paper towel or brown paper bag.

4. Stand each fried section upright on a table and with a heavy object smash it as flat as a pancake, using steady pressure rather than a sharp blow. (I use a small cutting board, but a frying pan will do fine.)

5. Put the smashed sections back into the hot oil, two or three at a time, and cook 2 minutes or so, until the entire surface is golden brown.

6. Remove, drain, and season them liberally with salt and pepper.

SERVES 4 AS A SIDE DISH

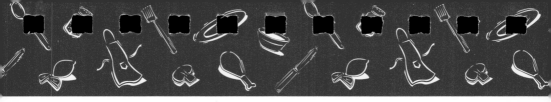

SIMPLE GRILLED WHOLE BEEF TENDERLOIN

HIGH

This cut of meat comes from the steer's back, a body part that gets very little exercise. This produces a very tender cut of meat, but one with little inherent flavor. Grilling, however, solves this problem without sacrificing the cut's melting tenderness. The heavy char that results from the grilling has its own delicious taste and crusty texture. To cook it properly on the grill takes a very moderate fire and lots of patience. I suggest having a fire in only half of the grill and placing the tenderloin where it is not directly over the heat.

This is a good dish to serve as part of a buffet, since the meat can be cut into small pieces and put on bread. I like to serve it with a couple of different condiments to complement the subtle beef flavor. The meat is also a great leftover, particularly in a salad with lemon and olive oil.

1 whole, unpeeled tenderloin of beef (5 to 6 pounds)
Salt and freshly cracked black pepper to taste

1. Trim the excess fat off the tenderloin and cover the meat heavily with salt and pepper to taste.

2. Over high heat, sear the tenderloin well on both sides. This will take about 10 to 12 minutes per side. Have your tongs ready, as a large flare-up may well occur. A flare-up in this situation actually aids in the searing process. If the flames are higher than 18 inches, though, I would take the tenderloin off and allow the flames to subside. In any case, large flame-ups tend to impress your guests. Always remain calm.

3. Remove the meat from the grill, then remove the grill and push your coals over to one side.

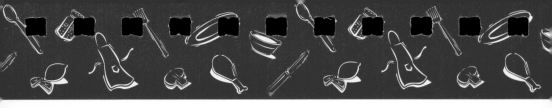

4. Replace the grill and put the tenderloin back on the grill, over the side with no coals.

5. Place the cover on the grill, and open the stop vent slightly, 1 to 2 inches or so.

6. Continue to cook, 25 minutes for rare meat, 30 minutes for medium rare.

7. Remove the meat from the grill and let it recline 15 minutes before serving (this lets the juices return from the center of the meat, where they have retreated during cooking.)

8. Serve 2 slices per person.

SERVES 7 TO 8 AS A MAIN COURSE
SERVING SUGGESTIONS: I would serve this Your Basic Grilled Corn (recipe 96) and West Indies Breadfruit Salad (recipe 91). Also, use either a single condiment or a selection of them. This is a great vehicle for just about any condiment you like. Check out Very Aromatic Tomato-Ginger Jam (recipe 73), Pebre: Chilean Hot Sauce (recipe 80), or anything that strikes your fancy.

GRILLED BIG BLACK-AND-BLUE STEAK FOR TWO

MEDIUM-HIGH

The ultimate red meat experience. The beauty of this dish lies in its simplicity, and the key is to buy the highest-quality meat possible and let the huge steak shine through in its own natural glory.

Now, this might sound a little religious to some of you, but in my childhood eating grilled steak on Saturday nights was very close to a spiritual experience. My father would go to the butcher shop Saturday afternoon, get a steak big enough for the whole family, and bring it home, where I helped him grill it. When it came to food my folks did not make a lot of fuss over the children—we ate it the way they cooked it, and for that reason I developed at a very young age a fine appreciation for good steak cooked hard (some might say burned) on the outside and rare (meaning raw) on the inside. So I'm very fussy about the way steaks are prepared, and usually only have them at home.

There is a reason why steaks are served with baked potatoes and salad. I'm not sure what it is, and I never bothered to ask; it's just one of those things that feels so right. I like this recipe with a big showy red wine but have also been known to accompany it with a couple of cold ones.

1 giant 1½-inch-thick steak (choose one of the
*   following):*
*   1 2-pound boneless Delmonico*
*   or*
*   1 2½-pound T-bone*
*   or*
*   1 2½-pound porterhouse*
¼ cup olive oil
Kosher salt and freshly cracked black pepper to
*   taste*

1. Allow the steak to come to room temperature, then rub it with oil and salt and pepper to taste.

2. Over a medium-hot fire, grill the steak until the exterior is very brown, almost black, and very crusty, about 8 to 9 minutes per side. Some flare-ups might occur. If they do, remove the steak from the grill using long tongs, allow the fire to calm down, and place the steak back on the grill. To check for doneness, nick the meat on one side and look at the color. It will appear slightly rarer than it will actually be after resting.

3. Remove the steak from the fire, allow it to rest 5 minutes, and serve with a baked potato and green salad.

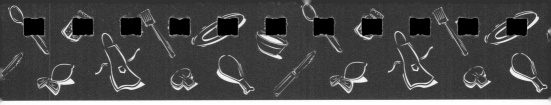

GRILLED PORK LOIN WITH INDONESIAN CHILE-COCONUT SAUCE

The chile-coconut sauce in this recipe is made from Asian staples that I saw used in many different ways when I visited Thailand. With the exception of the lemongrass, though, all of the ingredients could just as well come from Mexico. The cuisines of these two countries seem very different, but in fact they share many ingredients. When I created the recipe, I was thinking of mole sauce. I use the bitter chile taste characteristic of mole, but mellow it with coconut milk and sharpen it with aromatic lemongrass and lime juice.

FOR THE SAUCE (ABOUT 1½ CUPS)
10 ancho chile peppers
1 cup white vinegar
1 cup chicken stock
2 stalks lemongrass (see Pantry), minced (or 1 tablespoon dried)
4 tablespoons peeled and coarsely chopped fresh ginger
2 garlic cloves, peeled
1 tablespoon chopped cilantro
2 tablespoons lime juice (about 1 lime)
⅓ cup coconut milk (see Pantry)
Salt and freshly cracked black pepper to taste

8 pieces of pork loin (4 ounces each)

1. Soak the ancho chile peppers in water to cover for 12 hours. Drain them, pat them dry, seed them, and set them aside.

2. In a saucepan, combine the vinegar, chicken stock, lemongrass, and ginger. Bring to a boil, then lower the heat and simmer until it is reduced by one half, approximately 20 minutes. Strain the mixture and reserve, discarding the solids. Return the liquid to the saucepan.

3. Add the garlic and seeded anchos to the reserved liquid, simmer for 15 minutes, and purée in a food processor or blender.

4. Add the cilantro, lime juice, and coconut milk, and mix well. Season the mixture with salt and pepper to taste. Keeps up to 3 days, covered, in the refrigerator.

5. When you are ready to grill, place the pork pieces between two pieces of plastic wrap, and pound them until evenly thin but not torn.

6. Season the pork pieces with salt and pepper to taste, and grill them over high heat. If the pork is thin and your fire is hot, this should take about 2 minutes per side.

7. Serve 2 pieces of pork per person, partially covered by a couple of tablespoons of the Chile-Coconut Sauce.

SERVES 4 AS A MAIN COURSE

SERVING SUGGESTIONS: If you were out on the Pacific Rim, you would probably be eating this with the Spicy Cucumber Relish (recipe 74). I would suggest Sweet Potato Hash Browns with Bacon and Onions (recipe 92) to complete the meal.

WHEN IS THE PORK DONE?

◆

We all remember those pork chops from our youth—gray as a February day, dry as sawdust, and tasteless as the proverbial shoe leather. Fear of trichinosis, of course, was the culprit. Today, however, many cooks refuse to overcook pork, preferring to serve it pink to rosy-gray. Personally, I agree with them. While trichinosis has not been totally eliminated, it is certainly significantly less of a problem: There were only twenty-six cases in the United States in 1986, for example, in which pork was unequivocally the cause. The risk of eating less-than-well-done pork, in other words, seems to be no more than the danger of eating soft-boiled eggs, raw shellfish, or rare chicken. Some think it is worth the chance, others don't. Only you can be the judge.

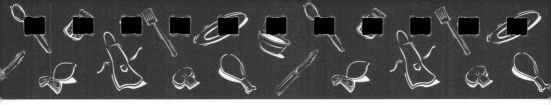

GRILLED PORK SKEWERS
WITH GREEN MANGO

It was in Burmese cuisine that I first ran across the idea of using green mango as a meat tenderizer. I like to use pork butt here so I can see how well the green mango does its job. The marinade also imparts a unique flavor.

2 pounds boneless pork butt

FOR THE MARINADE
2 green mangoes
1 tablespoon crushed red pepper flakes
½ cup pineapple juice
1 tablespoon white vinegar
¼ teaspoon turmeric
¼ teaspoon ground cumin
¼ teaspoon curry powder
¼ teaspoon chili powder
1 tablespoon minced garlic

1 red bell pepper, seeded
1 large red onion
Salt and freshly cracked black pepper to taste

1. Cut the pork butt into 1-inch cubes and put them into a large shallow dish.

2. Make the marinade: Peel one green mango and slice the fruit away from the inner pit. Put the fruit into a blender or food processor with the pepper flakes, pineapple juice, vinegar, turmeric, cumin, curry powder, chili powder, and garlic, and purée well.

3. Pour the marinade over the pork cubes. Cover, refrigerate, and marinate for 4 to 5 hours.

4. Peel the second mango and cut the fruit away from the inner pit, making as close to 1-inch cubes as possible. Cut the red pepper into about 12 chunks, and the onion into 1-inch cubes.

5. Remove the meat from the marinade, leaving as much of the marinade clinging to it as possible. Discard the remaining marinade.

6. Thread the pork cubes and pieces of mango, red pepper, and onion on skewers in a pleasing array. Season with salt and pepper to taste.

7. Grill the skewers over medium heat until the pork is cooked, about 5 to 7 minutes per side. If the pork begins to get too brown, you may cover the skewers with a pie plate to aid in cooking.

SERVES 4 AS A MAIN COURSE

SERVING SUGGESTIONS: I'd recommend serving this on white rice accompanied by Very Aromatic Tomato-Ginger Jam (recipe 73).

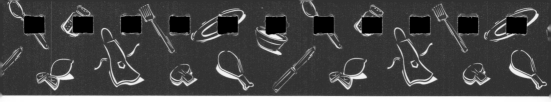

GRILLED PORK SKEWERS WITH GREEN TOMATOES AND YOUR SECRET FINISHING SAUCE

Here's a good use for those green tomatoes you have still hanging on the vines two days before the frost. "Finishing sauce" is a term used in barbecue, and it refers to a sauce that is brushed on just before meat is removed from the grill. Just a minute or two before you are ready to take the skewers off, brush this sauce on, let it caramelize a little, and the dish is ready. If you're having some fancy friends to dinner, tell them that the recipe for this sauce was given to you by an old man you met while traveling in Central America, that it has been handed down from father to son in his family, and you would never part with it. This dish is rather spicy and good served with tortillas.

FOR THE FINISHING SAUCE
1 teaspoon ground achiote seed (see Pantry)
*   (you may substitute paprika)*
1 teaspoon ground cumin
1 teaspoon chili powder
2 tablespoons balsamic vinegar
1 tablespoon molasses
1 tablespoon chopped fresh oregano
Juice of 1 orange
2 tablespoons lime juice (about 1 lime)
Salt and freshly cracked black pepper to taste

FOR THE SKEWERS
2½-pound pork butt
1 pound green tomatoes (about 4 tomatoes)
2 large yellow onions

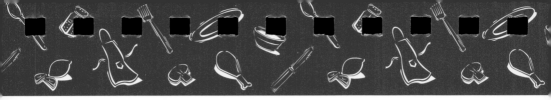

1. Combine all the Finishing Sauce ingredients in a saucepan, bring to a boil, and simmer over low heat for 5 minutes.

2. Remove the sauce from the heat. What you don't use for this recipe will keep, covered in the refrigerator, for about 2 weeks.

3. Cut the pork, tomatoes, and onions into chunks ¼-inch in diameter and thread them alternately on skewers.

4. Place the skewers on the grill over high heat and sear well. This should take about 3 to 4 minutes per side. Just before the meat is pulled off the grill, hit it with your secret sauce. Leave the skewers over the heat long enough to get some color, then pull them off.

SERVES 4 AS A MAIN COURSE

SERVING SUGGESTIONS: Serve this with Your Basic Black Beans (recipe 95) or Sweet Potato Salad (recipe 93). You might try putting Tropical Gazpacho (recipe 1) in front of it.

GRILLED PORK BIRDIES WITH TANGERINE-ROSEMARY GLAZE

MEDIUM-HIGH

The distinctly earthy flavor of fresh rosemary always reminds me of fall, and I see this dish being grilled out in the backyard among the fallen leaves and early sunsets that follow Indian summer.

This recipe calls for boneless pork loin, sometimes known as cutlets or fillets or, as my grandmother always called them, pork birdies. The meat is tender and flavorful and is complemented well by the sweet tangerine sauce with the dominant aromatic rosemary flavor. If fresh rosemary is not available, substitute fresh oregano or thyme rather than dried rosemary, which has a quite different flavor from fresh.

FOR THE GLAZE
¼ cup sugar
½ cup white vinegar
1 cup fresh tangerine juice (about 3 tangerines)
  (you may substitute fresh orange juice)
1 tablespoon fresh rosemary needles
1 tablespoon lime juice (about ½ lime)
Salt and freshly cracked black pepper to taste
2 tablespoons unsalted butter

8 4-ounce boneless pork birdies (loin fillets)
Salt and freshly cracked black pepper to taste

1. In a saucepan over medium heat, boil the sugar and vinegar together for 5 minutes. Add the tangerine juice and simmer until reduced by a third to a half. At this point the mixture should coat the back of a wooden spoon.

2. Remove the mixture from the heat, add the rosemary, lime juice, and salt and pepper to taste. Mix well, then add the butter and stir gently until it is melted and well incorporated.

3. Rub the birdies with salt and pepper to taste and place them on the grill over

medium-high heat for 3 to 4 minutes per side. The surface of the meat should be slightly brown and crispy, and the interior should have a hint of pinkness, depending on your preference. (Check the interior by nicking one of the birdies slightly with a knife). If you like yours cooked completely through, leave it on an additional 2 minutes per side.) Spoon the glaze generously over the grilled birdies before serving.

SERVES 4 AS A MAIN COURSE

SERVING SUGGESTIONS: Accompany this with Your Basic Grilled Corn (recipe 96).

GRILLED PORK TENDERLOIN WITH ROASTED CORN-BACON RELISH

MEDIUM

The tenderloin is the tenderest cut of pork, suitable for grilling because its large surface area allows it to acquire a good amount of exterior char. Its subtle flavor combines well with the mellow but distinct taste of the relish. As for the corn, there are many ways to grill it on the cob, the main consideration being the degree of grilled/charred flavor you want. Here we want a lot, so we encourage it by glazing the ear of corn with maple syrup while it's on the grill.

FOR THE RELISH
3 ears of corn, shucked
4 tablespoons maple syrup
3 slices of bacon, diced small
1 large yellow onion, diced small
1 teaspoon chopped fresh sage
Salt and freshly cracked black pepper to taste

3 pork tenderloins (10- to 12- ounces each)
Salt and freshly cracked black pepper to taste

1. Cook the corn in boiling water for 4 minutes. Remove it and allow to cool to room temperature.

2. Over a medium fire, grill the corn 2 to 3 minutes, or until lightly brown. Brush on the maple syrup and continue to grill for an additional 2 to 3 minutes, or until the syrup begins to caramelize (it will turn golden brown). Remove the corn from the grill and cool.

3. With a sharp knife, remove the kernels from the cob.

4. In a sauté pan, cook the bacon over medium heat until crisp, about 5 minutes. Add the onion and cook an additional 4 to 5 minutes, or until the onion is clear. Add the corn and cook 2 minutes more.

5. Remove the corn mixture from the heat, add the sage, and season to taste with salt and pepper. Stir well and set aside.

6. Rub the tenderloins with salt and pepper to taste and grill them over a medium fire for 12 to 15 minutes, rolling them every 3 to 4 minutes to ensure even cooking. (I prefer to eat this cut slightly pink, but if you like yours cooked completely, leave it on an additional 4 to 5 minutes.)

7. Remove the tenderloins from the grill, allow them to stand for 5 minutes, then carve each into ½-inch slices. Spoon some relish over each portion of the sliced pork and serve.

SERVES 4 AS A MAIN COURSE

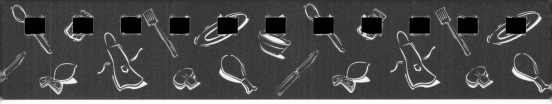

GRILLED WEST INDIES SPICE-RUBBED CHICKEN BREAST WITH GRILLED BANANA

This is a variation for the grill of the dry rub commonly used in barbecue. The normal searing and crusting action of grilling is enhanced by the rub, and the result is a supercrusted, flavor-concentrated surface covering a moist breast. The grilled banana provides a little sweetness and mellowness to contrast with the crispy chicken.

FOR THE SPICE RUB
3 tablespoons curry powder
3 tablespoons ground cumin
2 tablespoons allspice
3 tablespoons paprika
2 tablespoons powdered ginger
1 tablespoon cayenne pepper
2 tablespoons salt
2 tablespoons freshly cracked black pepper
4 boneless chicken breasts, skin on

4 firm bananas, skin on and halved lengthwise
2 tablespoons vegetable oil
1 tablespoon soft butter
2 tablespoons molasses
Lime halves for garnish

1. Mix all the spices together well, rub this mixture over both sides of each chicken breast, cover, and refrigerate for 2 hours.

2. Over a medium fire, grill the chicken breasts skin-side down for 7 to 8 minutes, until well browned and heavily crusted. Turn them and grill an additional 10 minutes. Check for doneness by nicking the largest breast at the fattest point: The meat should be fully opaque with no traces of red. Remove the chicken from the grill.

3. Rub the banana halves with vegetable oil and place them on the grill,

flat-side down. Grill them for about 2 minutes, or until the flat sides are slightly golden in color. Flip them and grill for an additional 2 minutes.

4. Remove the banana halves from the grill. Mix the butter and molasses together and paint this over the bananas. Serve the chicken breasts and banana halves together, sprinkled with a little lime juice.

SERVES 4 AS A MAIN COURSE

SERVING SUGGESTIONS: I might put a pat of butter on each breast and serve them with Black Bean Salad (recipe 95).

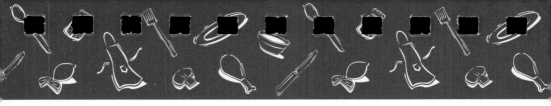

GRILLED JAMAICAN JERK CHICKEN WITH BANANA-GUAVA KETCHUP

◆

JAMAICAN JERK RUB

In my surfing days, I stumbled upon a beach near Port Antonio, Jamaica, called Boston Bay. It turned out to have decent waves, but more significantly to be the best place on the island for jerk chicken and jerk pork. Originally created by escaped Maroon slaves as a method of preserving pork by rubbing it with a paste and then open-pit smoking it, this uniquely Jamaican dish has evolved into pork and chicken that is rubbed with the same mixture and then grilled slowly so that it dries out. The paste is the foundation of this dish and its key ingredient is the infamous Scotch Bonnet pepper (known as the habañero pepper). Scotch Bonnet chile peppers are difficult to find fresh, although sometimes you can pick them up in Spanish markets where Caribbean and South American products are sold. It is easier to find the traditional hot Caribbean table sauce that uses the Scotch Bonnet as its main ingredient. The wildly aromatic taste is unique and unmistakable and the sauce is exceptionally hot.

Here are two versions of the recipe, one using fresh Scotch Bonnet chile peppers and the other using the bottled sauce.

I like to use chicken thighs in this dish because they have center bones and so can withstand the long cooking time on the grill and still be juicy. If you prefer serving boneless chicken, it's very easy to remove the one bone from the thigh before serving.

FOR THE RUB
¼ cup Inner Beauty (see Pantry) or other
   Caribbean hot sauce or 10 puréed Scotch
   Bonnet chile peppers (you may substitute
   15 of your favorite fresh chile peppers)
2 tablespoons dried rosemary

2 tablespoons parsley, chopped
2 tablespoons dried basil
2 tablespoons dried thyme
2 tablespoons mustard seeds
3 scallions, finely chopped
1 teaspoon salt
1 teaspoon black pepper
Juice of 2 limes
¼ cup cheap yellow mustard
2 tablespoons orange juice
2 tablespoons white vinegar

6 chicken thighs, with legs attached

1. Combine all the rub ingredients in a food processor or blender, and blend them into a paste, making sure that all the ingredients are fully integrated. The paste should be approximately the consistency of a thick tomato sauce. If it is too thick, thin it out with a little more white vinegar.

2. Cover the paste and let it sit in the refrigerator for at least 2 hours for the flavors to blend together. Overnight is the ideal amount of time to give them to get acquainted.

3. Rub the chicken thighs with the paste and place them on the grill over very low heat. If you have a covered cooker, put the coals to one side, the chicken on the other, and cover.

4. Cook about 1 hour without a cover or ½ hour if covered. The key here is to use a very low heat. You need to be patient and give yourself plenty of time. The chicken is technically done when the meat is opaque and the juices run clear. However, the ideal is about 10 to 15 minutes past that point, when the meat pulls away from the bone easily. It is very hard to overcook this. In fact you can only screw it up if you burn the paste by having the heat too high. The longer the chicken stays on the grill, the more superior the smoky flavor.

5. After cooking, separate the leg from the thigh by cutting at the natural joint between them. Serve one leg or thigh per person accompanied by a few spoonfuls of Banana-Guava Ketchup.

SERVES 4 AS AN ENTRÉE OR 6 AS A
LIGHT MEAL

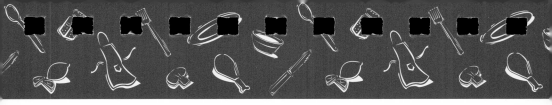

BANANA-GUAVA KETCHUP

Banana-guava ketchup is certainly not a traditional accompaniment to jerk chicken, but the ingredients reproduce the authentic spirit of the dish and the sweet richness of the ketchup helps people who need a cool taste against the chicken.

I use guava paste in the dish. If you can't find it in your local Spanish or Portuguese store, just leave it out—the bananas can carry the flavor.

1 yellow onion, diced
2 tablespoons vegetable oil
5 ripe bananas (anywhere from totally yellow to spotted brown) (about 2 pounds), peeled and broken into pieces
4 ounces (½ cup) guava paste combined with 1 cup orange juice or 1 12-ounce can guava nectar [you may substitute 8 ounces (1 cup) of guava jelly combined with ½ cup of orange juice]
2 tablespoons brown sugar
2½ tablespoons raisins
1 tablespoon curry powder
½ cup fresh orange juice
2 tablespoons white vinegar
4 tablespoons lime juice (about 2 limes)
Salt and freshly cracked black pepper to taste

1. In a heavy-bottomed pan over medium heat, sauté the onion in vegetable oil until transparent, about 5 to 7 minutes.

2. Add the banana pieces to the pan and cook over moderate heat for about 5 minutes, stirring constantly to avoid sticking.

3. Add the guava paste mixture, brown sugar, raisins, curry powder, orange juice, and 1 tablespoon vinegar. Bring to a boil and simmer for about 15 minutes. The mixture should have the consistency of applesauce when hot, but will firm up as it cools.

4. Remove from the heat and stir in the remaining tablespoon of vinegar, the lime juice, and salt and pepper to taste. You may serve this hot or at room temperature. It will keep, covered and refrigerated, up to 6 weeks.

2 CUPS

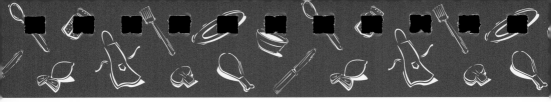

GRILLED CHICKEN BREAST WITH FRESH HERBS AND LEMON

This dish is representative of what much of today's cooking is moving toward: a simple yet high-quality preparation where the ingredients stand on their own. Dishes that highlight the food, not the cook. I use a boneless breast because in the absence of saintlike patience I find it impossible to cook a bone-in chicken breast on an open grill. Any fresh herb or combination of herbs works fine for this dish—the key word is "fresh." I would choose from thyme, basil, oregano, parsley, and rosemary.

4 boneless chicken breasts, skin on
Salt and freshly cracked black pepper to taste
¼ cup chopped mixed fresh herbs
¼ cup virgin olive oil
8 tablespoons lemon juice (about 2 lemons)

1. Rub the breasts all over with salt and pepper to taste and grill them skin-side down over a medium fire for 10 to 12 minutes. The skin should be quite crisp.

2. While the breasts are grilling, combine the mixed herbs, olive oil, and lemon juice in a small bowl until well blended.

3. Turn the breasts and grill for an additional 5 to 6 minutes. During the last minute of cooking, brush the herb mixture on both sides of the chicken.

4. Remove the chicken from the grill and check for doneness by cutting into the thickest part: There should be no pink color and the flesh should be consistently opaque.

SERVES 4 AS A MAIN COURSE

SERVING SUGGESTIONS: I would accompany this straightforward dish with Black Bean Salad (recipe 95).

CHICKEN HOBO PACK

MEDIUM

DEDICATED TO THE BOYS
OF THE LONGHORN PATROL, TROOP 103

The hobo pack takes its place alongside a tuna fish sandwich and Jell-O as one of my earliest recipes. As the newest member of the Longhorn Patrol of my local Boy Scout troop, I was elected to be the cook on our camping trip. Unsure of what to prepare for the guys, I was forced to rely on an old Boy Scout favorite that consists of vegetables, potatoes, hamburger, and a huge amount of ketchup wrapped up in foil and put in the burning embers of the campfire. The guys loved it.

Along with the rest of my cooking repertoire, the hobo pack has evolved over the years and is now a constant menu item on day trips to the beach. The combination convection/conduction cooking method, in which the food is surrounded by coals and slow-cooked, makes it a very easy affair. You can use this method with all kinds of ingredients, but I like it with chicken and lots of garlic, which mellows when it cooks and merges with all the juice from the chicken. The packs can be made up ahead and refrigerated for 4 to 8 hours.

1 3-pound chicken, cut in half
1 large sweet potato, quartered
*1 whole head of garlic, unpeeled and sliced in
    half horizontally*
1 large onion, quartered
1 large ripe tomato, quartered
1 ear of corn, husked and cut into 4 pieces
1 medium carrot, cut into large chunks
2 rosemary sprigs
Salt and freshly cracked black pepper to taste
4 tablespoons butter

1. Lay one chicken half on a large sheet of extra-heavy-duty tinfoil. Arrange half of the vegetables over and around the chicken, add 1 sprig rosemary, and salt and

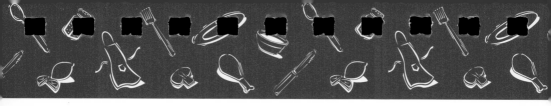

pepper to taste, dot 2 tablespoons of butter over all, and put another large sheet of tinfoil on top. Roll the edges of the two sheets together, closing the pack. Fold the edges up, making sure you remember which side is up. Now cover the entire pack with one more layer of tinfoil.

2. Repeat with the second chicken half and remaining ingredients.

3. It's best to use a campfire where you have plenty of room to work, but a large grill will do as well. Build a medium fire, place the packs on the bottom of the fire or grill, top-side up, and arrange coals all around them. Make sure to keep hot burning coals constantly around the packs, and cook for 30 to 45 minutes, depending upon the intensity of your heat.

4. Remove the packs from the coals, unroll the tinfoil, and catch the wonderful smell. For the full hobo pack experience, sit on the ground and eat it out of the tinfoil with Cokes and candy bars, then play a game of Capture the Flag and tell ghost stories. It is also okay to serve it on a plate with some crusty bread for the juices, a salad, and a bottle of white wine—but then some people have no respect for culinary traditions.

SERVES 2

SERVING SUGGESTIONS: Serve this with Girl Scout cookies and that nice ice-cold beer you couldn't have when you were a Boy Scout.

GRILLED TURKEY STEAKS WITH WHITE GRAPE-CRANBERRY RELISH

Turkey fillets work well on the grill, since the quick cooking method retains the moistness of the interior meat while the fire gives more flavor to the exterior surface. Most supermarkets now carry boneless turkey breast cut into fillets, scallops, or steaks, which are all basically the same cut. The tang of the cranberry balances the sweetness of the grapes in the relish, for a nontraditional traditional combination.

FOR THE RELISH
½ cup fresh cranberries
½ cup blush or rosé wine
3 tablespoons sugar
½ cup orange juice
1 pound seedless white grapes, halved
2 tablespoons lime juice (about 1 lime)

4 10-ounce turkey fillets (about ½-inch thick)
Salt and freshly cracked black pepper to taste

1. Make the relish: In a saucepot over low heat, bring the cranberries, wine, and sugar to a boil, stirring until the sugar is dissolved. Add the orange juice and half of the grapes, reduce the heat, and simmer for 5 minutes.

2. Remove from the heat, add the rest of the grapes and the lime juice, mix well, and allow to cool. Will keep, covered and refrigerated, up to 2 weeks.

3. Rub the fillets on both sides with salt and pepper to taste and cook them over a medium-hot fire for about 4 to 5 minutes per side. Check for doneness by nicking one side; the meat should be opaque throughout. Remove them from grill and serve with the relish.

SERVES 4 AS A MAIN COURSE

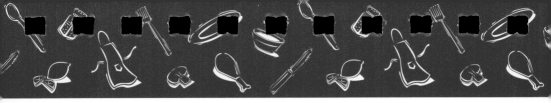

GRILLED MARINATED QUAIL

I like food that I can eat with my hands, food that has a lot of bones in it, and that requires a lot of lip smacking to eat properly. A knife and fork simply do not do justice to this dish. I'd serve it plain with some hunks of bread, lemons for squeezing, and extra virgin olive oil for drizzling.

6 quail
1 tablespoon minced garlic
1 tablespoon fresh rosemary leaves
Salt and freshly cracked black pepper to taste
4 tablespoons olive oil
4 tablespoons red wine vinegar
2 lemons, cut into wedges, for garnish
4 tablespoons chopped parsley
3 tablespoons capers

1. Butterfly the quail.

2. Rub the butterflied quail with the garlic, rosemary, and salt and pepper to taste, and place them skin-side down in a shallow pan.

3. Pour the oil and vinegar over the quail, and let stand for 3 to 4 hours.

4. Remove the quail from the pan, and grill them over medium-high heat for 6 to 8 minutes per side. They should be cooked through, but pinkish in appearance.

5. Serve the quail on a platter garnished with lemon wedges and sprinkled with parsley and capers.

SERVES 6 AS AN APPETIZER

SERVING SUGGESTIONS: Serve this with Grilled Expensive Mushrooms on Texas Toast (recipe 4) as an appetizer, and accompany it with a relish or sauce such as Tangerine-Tamarind Sauce (recipe 81), Black Olive and Citrus Relish (recipe 70), or my personal favorite, Raisin-Ginger Chutney (recipe 65).

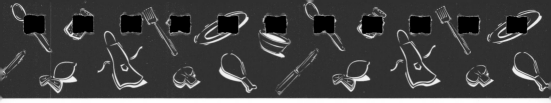

GRILLED VENISON LOIN WITH BOURBON PEACHES

The loin is part of the deer that receives little exercise, and thus is a very tender and not overly gamy-tasting cut of meat. This dish is a good one for introducing someone to venison. When properly cooked, the loin bears a strong taste resemblance to fine aged beef. As opposed to most other cuts of venison, which require long periods of cooking to tenderize the meat, the loin is at its best when cooked quickly and served rare. Sounds like you might want to grill it, doesn't it?

I wouldn't want to serve any sauce with this; it should be enjoyed for its subtle richness. Slightly tart, sweet pickled peaches make a wonderful accompaniment. You might want to pickle the peaches during the summer, then serve them with the venison in the late fall, as it is more seasonally appropriate.

1 2¼ -pound venison loin, cut into 2 pieces
Salt and freshly cracked black pepper to taste

1. Season the venison steaks with salt and pepper to taste on both sides, and grill them over a medium-hot fire for 5 to 6 minutes per side, until well-seared. Remove and allow them to rest for 5 minutes, then slice them thinly. If you find them too rare, put the slices back on the grill for a minute.

SERVES 5 AS A MAIN COURSE

SERVING SUGGESTIONS: I recommend trying Sweet Potato Hash Browns with Bacon and Onions (recipe 92) and plain steamed green beans or Your Basic Grilled Corn (recipe 96) as side dishes with this.

BOURBON PEACHES

1 cup sugar
1½ cups water
1 cup cider vinegar
8 small peaches, quartered and pitted
10 cloves
½ cup bourbon
4 fresh mint sprigs

1. Combine the sugar, water, and vinegar in a saucepan, and bring to a boil, stirring until the sugar dissolves.

2. Add the peaches and cloves, simmer for 5 minutes, then remove from the heat.

3. Allow this to cool to room temperature, then pour it into a quart jar. Add the bourbon and mint, cover tightly, and refrigerate for at least 1 week. Will keep for up to 6 weeks covered airtight and refrigerated.

SAMBALS, BLATJANGS, AND SALSAS

BANANA-GREEN MANGO CHUTNEY

Your basic chutney. The sweetish taste of this condiment delivers an excellent balance to very hot dishes.

1 large yellow onion, diced small
2 tablespoons peanut oil
1 green (unripe) mango, peeled and diced small
1 cup white vinegar
1 cup fresh orange juice
1 pound very ripe bananas, sliced ¼-inch thick
1 tablespoon grated fresh ginger
½ cup raisins
½ cup packed dark brown sugar
1 tablespoon finely chopped fresh serrano or
    jalapeño chile peppers (you may substitute
    ¾ tablespoon red pepper flakes)
Salt and freshly cracked black pepper to taste
1 teaspoon allspice

1. Sauté the onion in the oil until clear, 4 to 5 minutes.

2. Add the mango and cook 2 minutes over medium heat.

3. Add the vinegar and orange juice, bring to a simmer, and simmer for 10 minutes.

4. Add all the remaining ingredients and bring the mixture back to a simmer.

5. As soon as a simmer is reached, remove the mixture from the heat, cool to room temperature, and serve. This will keep, covered and refrigerated, for up to 2 weeks.

ABOUT 5 CUPS

SERVING SUGGESTIONS: Serve this with Grilled Pork Skewers with Green Tomatoes and Your Secret Finishing Sauce (recipe 52) or Grilled West Indies Spice-Rubbed Chicken Breast with Grilled Banana (recipe 55).

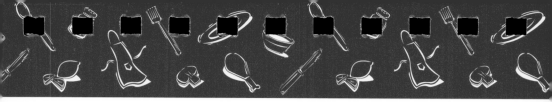

PEAR-CRANBERRY CHUTNEY

◆

This chutney has a Day-Glo translucency that is almost psychedelic, an interesting consistency, and goes well with grilled ham, turkey, or chicken. Perfect for an unusual holiday condiment.

1 large yellow onion, diced small
2 tablespoons vegetable oil
4 firm pears of any kind, peeled, cored, and
    diced small
Juice of 2 oranges
¼ cup fresh cranberries
A pinch each of cinnamon, powdered ginger,
    and allspice

1. In a saucepot, sauté the onion in the oil over medium heat until clear, about 4 minutes.

2. Add the diced pear and orange juice. Bring to a simmer, and add the cranberries and spices. Stirring frequently, simmer until the cranberries start to burst, then remove the mixture from the heat. It should have the consistency of wet sand. Keeps, covered and refrigerated, up to 2 weeks.

ABOUT 2 CUPS

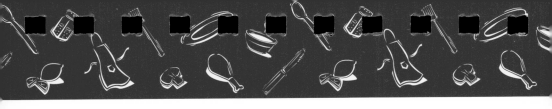

COCONUT AND LEMONGRASS CHUTNEY

◆

This collection of Southeast Asian ingredients and flavors has a wonderful variety of textures. It has the unique ability to be served with subtle fish dishes and not overpower them, even though it is super-spicy.

1 cup fresh grated coconut
4 tablespoons minced fresh lemongrass (see Pantry) or 1 tablespoon dried
2 tablespoons minced fresh ginger
¼ cup roasted, unsalted peanuts
8 tablespoons lime juice (about 4 limes)
4 tablespoons honey
2 tablespoons chopped fresh mint
2 tablespoons chopped cilantro
1 tablespoon fresh red or green hot chile pepper, minced

1. Grate the coconut into a medium-sized bowl. Add the lemongrass and ginger, and mix.

2. Chop the peanuts coarsely and add to the mixture. Add the lime juice and honey, and mix lightly.

3. Toss in the mint, cilantro, and hot chile, and stir a couple of times to integrate them. Keeps, covered and refrigerated, 4 days.

ABOUT 2 CUPS

SERVING SUGGESTIONS: This is particularly good with rather heavy fish. Try it with a plain grilled kingfish or tuna.

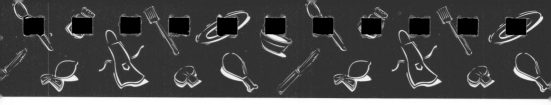

RAISIN-GINGER CHUTNEY

◆

This very potent condiment is particularly outstanding with grilled country ham. A friend of mine who loves spicy food has taken to using this as a spread on pita bread, which he claims makes a great lunch.

1 medium yellow onion, diced small
2 tablespoons peanut oil
½ pound raisins
2 tablespoons minced fresh ginger
2 teaspoons minced garlic
1½ teaspoons red pepper flakes
1½ teaspoons curry powder
1½ teaspoons brown sugar
½ cup orange juice
2 tablespoons cider vinegar
Salt and freshly cracked black pepper to taste

1. In a sauté pan, sauté the diced onion in the peanut oil over moderate heat until clear, 5 to 7 minutes.

2. Add the raisins, ginger, garlic, red pepper flakes, and curry powder, and cook over low to medium heat, stirring frequently, for 4 minutes.

3. Add the brown sugar and orange juice, and continue to cook over low heat for 10 minutes.

4. Add the vinegar and salt and pepper to taste, and bring to a boil. Lower the heat and simmer for 5 minutes.

5. Remove from the heat and cool to room temperature before serving. Keeps, in a closed container and refrigerated, up to 5 weeks.

ABOUT 2 CUPS

GEORGIA PEACH CHUTNEY

H ere's another example of that classic tropical combination of sweet fruit and acid. The sweetness in this chutney comes from the American South in the form of peaches and molasses, and combining them with vinegar and lemon juice after cooking adds an extra jolt of tartness.

2 large yellow onions, diced small
1 to 2 tablespoons vegetable oil
4 peaches, each pitted and sliced into 16 slices
4 tablespoons packed brown sugar
4 tablespoons white sugar
1 tablespoon molasses
¼ cup raisins
1 teaspoon salt
½ teaspoon freshly cracked pepper (white is best if you have it)
¼ teaspoon allspice
½ cup white vinegar
2 tablespoons fresh lemon juice (about ½ lemon)

1. In a saucepot over medium heat, sauté the onion in the oil until transparent, about 5 to 7 minutes.

2. Add the peach slices, stir, and cook for 4 minutes.

3. Add all the remaining ingredients except ¼ cup of the vinegar and the lemon juice. Simmer uncovered over low heat for 1 hour, stirring occasionally and being very careful not to burn the mixture. If necessary, add a small amount of water to prevent the mixture from burning.

4. Remove the mixture from the heat, add the lemon juice and the other ¼ cup vinegar, and mix thoroughly. The chutney will have the texture of thick, chunky applesauce—it will be thinner than you expect, if you are used to Major Grey's.

5. Serve the chutney at room temperature. It will keep, tightly covered and refrigerated, for about 6 weeks.

ABOUT 3 CUPS

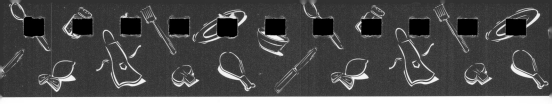

LEESBURG CHOWCHOW

A nother great use for those green tomatoes left in your garden at the end of the summer. This recipe was inspired by an old cookbook written by a Virginia housewife. Like most pickling recipes, it makes a large quantity. This makes sense, since the pickling process takes 3 days. Fortunately it stores very well and is an excellent condiment at any time of the year. It is particularly good with barbecue.

8 to 10 medium green tomatoes
12 cucumbers
1 medium head green cabbage
6 large yellow onions
2 cups kosher salt
6 cups water
6 cups white vinegar
8 cups cider vinegar
1 cup prepared horseradish
2 tablespoons celery seed
1 cup mustard seeds

4 tablespoons freshly ground black pepper
4 tablespoons turmeric
4 tablespoons cinnamon

1. Cut the tomatoes into eighths. Peel and deseed the cucumbers, and dice the cucumbers, cabbage, and onions into 1-inch cubes.

2. In a large bowl, toss the tomato, cucumber, cabbage, and onion with the 2 cups of kosher salt. Pack the mixture into a container with a weight on top to make sure the vegetables stay submerged. Refrigerate, covered, for 24 hours.

3. After 24 hours, rinse all the ingredients in a colander, return them to the container, and cover them with a mixture of equal parts water and white vinegar. Let them soak for 24 hours, covered and weighted. After 24 hours, rinse the mixture again.

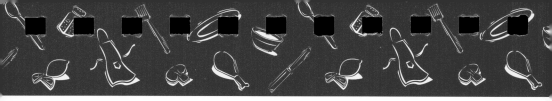

4. In a large stockpot, heat the cider vinegar until it just begins to boil. Remove it from the heat and add the horseradish, celery seed, mustard seeds, pepper, turmeric, and cinnamon. Mix well and pour this over the vegetable mixture.

5. Allow everything to marinate for another 24-hour period. You now have an official pickle. It will keep, covered and refrigerated, for the rest of your life, or you can can it and put it on the shelf.

ABOUT 1½ GALLONS

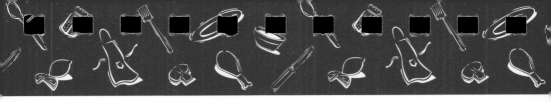

SMOKED APPLE-CHILE RELISH

The combination of the smoky flavor and spicy chile peppers is a natural, and somehow apples seem to fit right in— maybe it's because I associate burning leaves with apple season. This relish is perfect with pork.

4 ancho chile peppers
4 tablespoons white vinegar
12 Granny Smith apples
2 large yellow onions
4 tablespoons vegetable oil
4 tablespoons chili powder
2 tablespoons ground cumin
12 orange segments
2 tablespoons lemon juice (about ½ lemon)
Salt and freshly cracked black pepper to taste
1 tablespoon chopped fresh oregano

1. Soak the ancho chile peppers in hot water for 12 hours to reconstitute them.

2. In a food processor or blender, purée the chile peppers with the vinegar until completely puréed. Press the purée through a medium strainer. Discard the remaining skins, and reserve the purée.

3. Core and quarter the apples, leaving the skins on. Peel the onions and slice them into ½-inch slices. Lightly coat the apple and sprinkle them with 2 tablespoons each of the chili powder and cumin.

4. In a covered grill, build a small fire as far over to one side as possible. Wait for all of the fuel to be completely engulfed in flame.

5. Place the apple and onion slices on the grill on the side opposite the fire, cover the grill, and let it smoke for about 20 minutes. Check the tenderness of the apples: They should be slightly mushy on the outer surface, but still quite firm overall. Remove

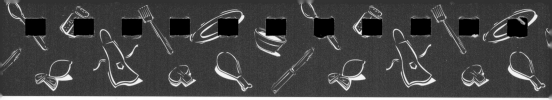

the apple slices from the heat and continue to smoke the onion slices with the cover on until cooked through, about 30 minutes in all.

6. Coarsely chop the apple and onion slices, and place them in a mixing bowl. Toss them with the remaining chili powder, orange segments, lemon juice, and the chile purée. Season with salt and pepper to taste and oregano. Will keep up to 4 days covered and refrigerated.

ABOUT 4 CUPS

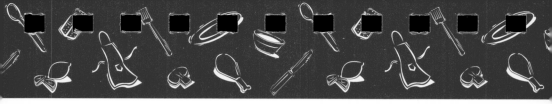

APRICOT BLATJANG

A "blatjang" (blaht-jahng) is a South African preserve traditionally served along with pickled vegetables to balance the heat of curries. It is very similar to Indian chutney, and it shows the strong influence of the cooking of the East Indian slaves who were brought to South Africa by the Dutch. Since blatjangs are strong enough to compete with curries, they can also stand up to the strong taste of grilled foods.

1 pound dried apricots
1 small yellow onion, diced small
¼ pound golden raisins
½ cup plus 4 tablespoons red wine vinegar
1 tablespoon minced garlic
2 tablespoons grated fresh ginger
1 teaspoon cayenne
¼ cup blanched almonds, toasted
Salt to taste

1. In a saucepan, combine the apricots, onion, raisins, and ½ cup of the vinegar with enough water to cover.

2. Bring to a boil and simmer for 15 to 20 minutes, stirring frequently, until the mixture is the thickness of honey. Be careful not to overcook the mixture, as it will thicken as it cools. Remove the mixture from heat.

3. In a food processor or blender, combine the garlic, ginger, cayenne, almonds, and salt to taste, and purée well.

4. Add the puréed spice mixture to the apricot mixture, and mix well. Stir in the remaining 4 tablespoons of vinegar. Will keep, covered and refrigerated, up to 3 weeks.

About 2 cups

SERVING SUGGESTIONS: This is good with any type of grilled satay.

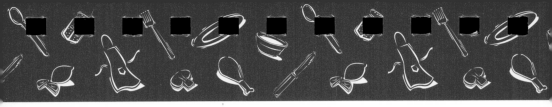

BLACK OLIVE AND CITRUS RELISH

◆

The sweet-sour taste of citrus makes a great combination with the rich, loamy taste of black olives. This relish is a variant of a North African condiment traditionally served with tagines and curries as well as with grilled meats.

2 oranges
2 lemons
½ cup pitted black olives, chopped into small pieces
1 small red onion, diced small
3 scallions, chopped
1 teaspoon ground cumin
¼ teaspoon cayenne pepper
Salt and freshly cracked black pepper to taste
2 tablespoons chopped parsley

1. Peel the oranges and lemons, separate them into sections, and remove the outer membranes and seeds.

2. Put the fruit into a medium-sized bowl, add all the remaining ingredients, and mix well. This will keep, covered and refrigerated, for about 4 days.
ABOUT 2 CUPS

SERVING SUGGESTIONS: Serve this with Grilled Chicken Breast with Fresh Herbs and Lemon (recipe 57) or alongside Grilled Basque Wings (recipe 12).

PICKLED LIMES WITH GINGER AND CHILES

In the summer, when limes are plentiful and cheap, get a batch and pickle 'em. Once that's done, you can chop them up to use as part of a chutney, add them to stews and curries as a flavor enhancer, or serve them by themselves with grilled fish.

10 limes, quartered
3 tablespoons kosher salt
4 tablespoons white vinegar
3 tablespoons grated fresh ginger
4 thinly sliced garlic cloves
5 or 6 of your favorite hot chile peppers, cut in half
½ cup sugar
5 to 6 fresh cilantro sprigs

1. Give the lime quarters one good squeeze, and reserve the juice for one of the many other recipes that call for it.

2. Combine the lime quarters with 2 tablespoons of the salt, mix thoroughly, and put the mixture in a tightly covered 1-quart glass (mason) jar.

3. Place the jar in a sunny window for 3 days.

4. After 3 days, mix in the remaining tablespoon of salt, replace the cover on the jar, and put the mixture in the back of your refrigerator for 4 to 6 weeks.

5. Pour the lime quarters and liquid from the jar into a saucepan, and bring to a simmer over low heat.

6. Add the vinegar, ginger, garlic, chile peppers, sugar, and cilantro. Mix well, then remove from the heat.

7. Cool the mixture to room temperature, then pour back into the jar. The limes will keep, covered tightly and refrigerated, for 6 weeks.

ABOUT 2 CUPS

SPICY BANANA-COCONUT KETCHUP

2 very ripe bananas
1 cup Indonesian Sweet Sauce (recipe 82)
⅓ cup coconut milk (see Pantry)
⅓ cup white vinegar
1 tablespoon minced fresh ginger
1 teaspoon Tabasco sauce

1. Mash or purée the bananas, then put them in a saucepan with the Indonesian Sweet Sauce. Cook over moderately high heat for 10 minutes.

2. Remove from the heat, add all the remaining ingredients, and mix until well blended. Keeps, covered and refrigerated, 1 week.

ABOUT 2 CUPS
SERVING SUGGESTIONS: This sweetish, exotic ketchup goes nicely with Grilled Pork Skewers with Green Mango (recipe 51), or Simple Grilled Whole Beef Tenderloin (recipe 48).

VERY AROMATIC
TOMATO-GINGER JAM

◆

The main features of this jam/condiment are its strength of flavor and the potent aromatic herb combination of lemongrass, basil, cilantro, and mint, which are added at the very end of the preparation so their flavors will emerge at full strength. I have encountered these herbs together in Vietnamese as well as Thai food. I find that this jam has a unique flavor that I'd serve with just about anything grilled.

1 medium yellow onion, very thinly sliced
3 tablespoons peanut oil
1 tablespoon minced garlic
2 tablespoons grated fresh ginger
2 large, ripe tomatoes, cut into small chunks
2 tablespoons sugar
2 tablespoons rice wine vinegar
1 tablespoon finely chopped scallion
1 tablespoon very finely chopped fresh lemon-
    grass (see Pantry) or 1 teaspoon dried

1 tablespoon finely chopped cilantro
1 tablespoon finely chopped basil
1 tablespoon finely chopped mint
2 tablespoons lime juice (about 1 lime)
2 tablespoons lemon juice (about ½ lemon)

1. In a large sauté pan over medium-high heat, sauté the onion slices in the peanut oil until well browned, 6 to 8 minutes. Add the garlic and ginger, and sauté 1 minute more.

2. Add the tomato and cook over low heat, stirring constantly, until the mixture is the consistency of wet sand, about 10 minutes. Be careful that the mixture does not stick to the pan.

3. Add the sugar and vinegar, and cook, stirring constantly, for an additional 2 minutes. Again, be careful not to let the mixture stick.

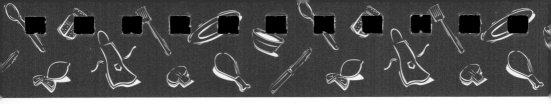

4. Remove from the heat and let cool 10 to 15 minutes.

5. Add the scallion, the herbs, and the lime and lemon juice, and stir until well blended. Will keep, covered and refrigerated, 10 days to 2 weeks.

ABOUT 2 CUPS

SERVING SUGGESTIONS: I might serve this as a condiment with Grilled Steamed Littlenecks Johnson (recipe 31), Simple Grilled Whole Beef Tenderloin (recipe 48), or Steamed Clams with Lemongrass and Chiles de Árbol (recipe 5).

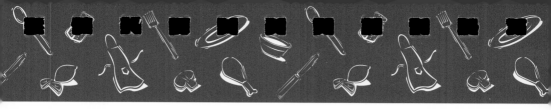

SPICY CUCUMBER RELISH

♦

Here's another illustration of the general rule that anything used in traditional Eastern cuisine as an accompaniment to curries is also very appropriate with grilled foods. This cucumber relish appears in Thai, Indonesian, Indian, and Vietnamese cuisines, each country adding its own touch. The best one I have tasted came from a street vendor in downtown Bangkok, and here is his recipe.

2 cucumbers
1 small red onion, diced
5 tablespoons white vinegar
4 tablespoons sugar
1 tablespoon chopped cilantro
1 teaspoon red pepper flakes
Salt and freshly cracked black pepper to taste

1. Wash the cucumbers well to remove the waxy deposit, cut them in half length-wise, and slice them thin.

2. In a bowl, mix all the remaining ingredients and toss the cucumber slices with the mixture. Will keep 4 days, covered and refrigerated.

ABOUT 2 CUPS

SERVING SUGGESTIONS: Serve this with Spice-Rubbed Grilled Monkfish (recipe 20), or Pasta from Hell (recipe 16).

BRAISED GARLIC AND ONION JAM

Although this may seem an unlikely pair of ingredients for a jam, the chemical reactions accomplished during their cooking make them a fantastic duo. When the onion browns, it means the sugar in the onion has caramelized. Likewise, when the garlic is roasted or braised, it mellows and becomes slightly sweet. This is a favorite of mine for grilled steaks. It's easy, quick, and keeps for weeks. Served hot or cold, it can be used almost anyplace.

4 tablespoons peanut oil
3 large yellow onions, very thinly sliced
1 large garlic bulb, braised (see Pantry)
2 tablespoons sugar
4 tablespoons balsamic vinegar
1 tablespoon fresh thyme
Salt and freshly cracked black pepper to taste

1. In a large sauté pan, heat the oil over high heat until very hot.

2. Turn the heat to medium and, being careful not to splash the oil, put in the onion and sauté, stirring constantly, until deep brown, about 8 to 10 minutes.

3. Add the garlic, sugar, and 2 tablespoons of the vinegar. Cook for 1 minute.

4. Remove from the heat, add the other 2 tablespoons of vinegar, the thyme, and salt and pepper to taste. Mix well and serve hot or cold. Keeps, covered and refrigerated, for up to 1 month.

ABOUT 1 CUP

SERVING SUGGESTIONS: This is a perfect accompaniment for any grilled red meat. Try it with Simple Grilled Whole Beef Tenderloin (recipe 48) or Grilled Big Black-and-Blue Steak for Two (recipe 49).

ROASTED RED PEPPER
COULIS WITH BASIL

This sauce is one of those accompaniments with a rich, intense flavor that can stand up to the hearty flavor that comes from grilling over wood. Excellent with any grilled seafood.

2 large yellow onions
3 tablespoons olive oil
6 roasted red bell peppers (see Pantry)
2 tablespoons braised garlic (see Pantry)
1 cup chicken stock
4 tablespoons balsamic vinegar
4 tablespoons lemon juice (about 1 lemon)
1 cup fresh basil leaves
Pinch of red pepper flakes
8 tablespoons virgin olive oil
Salt and freshly cracked black pepper to taste

1. Peel the onions, slice them into ½-inch slices, and rub them lightly with the 3 tablespoons of olive oil.

2. Place the onion slices on a grill over a medium-hot fire. Grill them for 2 or 3 minutes per side, until golden brown. Remove them from the grill.

3. Coarsely chop the peppers, garlic, and onion.

4. Place all the ingredients except the olive oil into a food processor and purée. When everything is fully puréed, slowly add the oil, with the food processor still running. Season with salt and pepper to taste, and use the sauce hot or cold. Will keep up to 6 days, covered and refrigerated.

ABOUT 3 CUPS

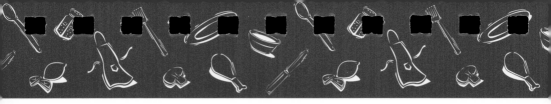

CHIPOTLE-MOLASSES GLAZE

◆

This is a combination of sweet, hot, and sour that has a distinctive flavor with a hint of smokiness. Good with game or a strong-charactered fish like bluefish or kingfish.

1 cup white vinegar
4 tablespoons sugar
1 cup fresh orange juice
4 tablespoons molasses
6 canned chipotles (see Pantry), puréed
4 tablespoons chopped cilantro
Salt and freshly cracked black pepper to taste
4 tablespoons lime juice (about 2 limes)

1. Combine the vinegar and sugar in a medium saucepan, bring to a boil, and simmer until reduced in volume by half, about 10 minutes.

2. Add the orange juice and again simmer until reduced in volume by half, about another 10 minutes

3. Remove from the heat, add the molasses, chipotle, and cilantro, and stir well. Season with salt and pepper to taste, and finish by adding the lime juice and mixing well. This will keep, covered air-tight and refrigerated, up to 3 weeks.

ABOUT 1 CUP

SERVING SUGGESTIONS: Try this with Grilled Venison Loin with Bourbon Peaches (recipe 61) or Lime-Marinated Grilled Kingfish with Red Onion and Mango Relish (recipe 21).

HOT ORANGE-CHILE GLAZE

A dandy flavor enhancer for any grilled duck or poultry. Try it with Grilled Chicken Breast with Fresh Herbs and Lemon (recipe 57), or Grilled Turkey Steaks with White Grape-Cranberry Relish (recipe 59).

2 tablespoons vegetable oil
1 medium yellow onion, chopped into small
    pieces
1 tablespoon chopped garlic
6 fresh green or red serrano chile peppers, diced
    small
2 tablespoons coriander seed
4 tablespoons chili powder
2 tablespoons ground cumin
Salt and freshly cracked black pepper to taste
1 cup orange juice
4 tablespoons molasses
1 cup vinegar
1 cup chicken stock
4 tablespoons cornstarch
4 tablespoons cold water
4 tablespoons chopped cilantro

1. In a heavy-bottomed saucepan, heat the oil until hot but not smoking. Cook the onion in the oil over medium heat until clear, 5 to 7 minutes. Add the garlic and serranos, and cook an additional 2 minutes.

2. Add the coriander seed, chili powder, cumin, salt and pepper to taste, orange juice, molasses, vinegar, and chicken stock, and bring this to a boil. Allow it to simmer for 20 minutes, stirring occasionally.

3. In a small bowl, mix the cornstarch and water together thoroughly. Slowly stir this mixture into the simmering glaze, making sure that it is thoroughly blended in. Continue to cook, and stir for an additional 10 minutes.

4. Remove the mixture from the heat and add the cilantro. Will keep, covered and refrigerated, 1 week to 10 days.

ABOUT 3 CUPS

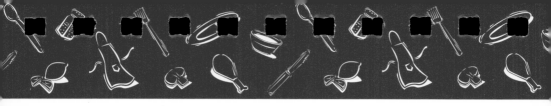

CLASSIC BRAZILIAN SAUCE

In Brazil, where grilled meats are very popular, there are many versions of simple sauces served as condiments, and often 2 or 3 different sauces will be served for sampling. This is one that I like to use on steaks. The heat is supplied by the serrano but you can substitute just about any heat.

6 fresh green or red serrano chile peppers
1 small yellow onion, diced
2 tablespoons chopped cilantro
1 tablespoon minced garlic
4 tablespoons olive oil
½ cup white vinegar
Salt and freshly cracked black pepper to taste

Combine all the ingredients in a food processor or blender, and purée. This sauce will keep, covered and refrigerated, for about 1 week.

ABOUT 1 CUP

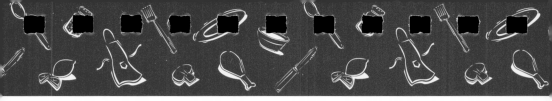

PEBRE: CHILEAN HOT SAUCE

In Chile, the genuine term for *salsa picante*, or hot sauce, is actually *pebre*. They do a lot of grilling in Chile, and they like it hot. This is your basic all-purpose grilled condiment.

3 tablespoons virgin olive oil
1 tablespoon spicy brown mustard
1 tablespoon white vinegar
4 tablespoons lime juice (about 2 limes)
1 red onion, diced small
2 scallions, diced
2 teaspoons Tabasco sauce or hot sauce of your choice
1 tablespoon minced garlic
Salt and freshly cracked black pepper to taste

   1. Stir the oil into the mustard. Add the vinegar and lime juice, and stir well.
   2. Add the red onion, scallion, Tabasco sauce, and garlic, and mix again. Season with salt and pepper to taste. This will be a rather thick sauce. Will keep, covered and refrigerated, for 4 to 6 weeks.

ABOUT 1 CUP

SERVING SUGGESTIONS: Serve this with Grilled Marinated Quail (recipe 60) or Grilled Venison Loin with Bourbon Peaches (recipe 61).

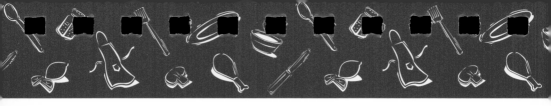

TANGERINE-TAMARIND SAUCE

◆

The tamarind is an exotic fruit indigenous to certain tropical climates. Sweet, sour, pungent, it is an excellent complement to spicy foods. I kind of fell upon this recipe, which allows the tamarind to come through in a subtle manner, when I misordered and was stuck with a full case of tangerines. I made the sauce, served it with squid and other seafood, and it has become a favorite of mine. I think you'll find that a squeeze of lime goes well with whatever you put the sauce on.

1 cup white vinegar
½ cup sugar
Peels of 3 tangerines
1 tablespoon minced fresh ginger
Juice of 10 tangerines
1 tablespoon tamarind paste (see Pantry)

1. In a saucepan, bring the vinegar and sugar to a boil. Add the tangerine peels and ginger, and simmer until the liquid is reduced by a half, about 15 minutes. Remove from the heat, strain the liquid into a bowl, and discard the peels and ginger.

2. Return the liquid to the saucepan, add the tangerine juice and tamarind paste, bring to a simmer, and reduce by a half to a third, about 20 minutes. Remove the sauce from the heat and allow it to cool to room temperature. Keeps, covered and refrigerated, up to 2 weeks.

ABOUT 1½ CUPS

SERVING SUGGESTIONS: Serve this on top of Grilled West Indies Spice-Rubbed Chicken Breast with Grilled Banana (recipe 55) or Grilled Pork Skewers with Green Mango (recipe 51).

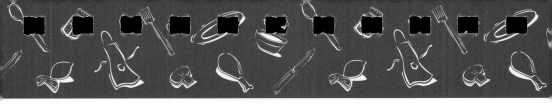

INDONESIAN SWEET SAUCE

This sauce is to Indonesian food what ketchup is to American food.

1 cup water
½ cup rice wine vinegar
½ cup brown sugar
1 tablespoon cornstarch
1 tablespoon water
½ cup soy sauce
⅓ cup molasses
Freshly cracked black pepper to taste

1. Bring the water and vinegar to a boil. Stir in the brown sugar and cook, stirring constantly, until the sugar dissolves.

2. Mix the cornstarch and water together well, and add this to the vinegar-sugar mixture. Continue to cook for an additional 3 minutes, until thickened.

3. Remove from the heat, add the soy sauce, molasses, and black pepper to taste, and stir well. Keeps, refrigerated, 3 weeks.

ABOUT 2 CUPS

WILD VARIATIONS

For the flavors of the Pacific Rim, add one of these sets of ingredients to 1 cup of the basic sauce.

1 tablespoon minced garlic
1 tablespoon minced fresh lemongrass (see Pantry) or 1 teaspoon dried
2 tablespoons minced hot fresh green or red chile peppers

6 tablespoons lime juice (about 3 limes)
3 tablespoons chopped cilantro
1 tablespoon red pepper flakes

1 tablespoon shrimp paste
1 tablespoon minced garlic
2 tablespoons chopped fresh basil
8 tablespoons lemon juice (about 2 lemons)

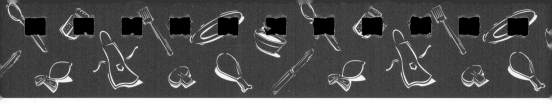

GINGER-LIME VINAIGRETTE

This vinaigrette has a very vibrant, aromatic flavor which is great with green salads. I also highly recommend it for any fresh garden vegetable or a simple grilled fish.

2 pieces of fresh ginger, each the size of your thumb, freshly peeled
12 tablespoons lime juice (about 6 limes)
4 tablespoons rice wine vinegar
½ red bell pepper, seeded and diced small
¼ red onion, diced small
4 tablespoons chopped cilantro
1 teaspoon grated lime rind
2 cups vegetable oil
Salt and freshly cracked black pepper to taste (white is best if you have it)

1. Place the ginger in a small saucepan and cover with cold water. Bring to a boil, drain, and repeat the procedure. Cool the ginger under cold tap water. (This will give it a milder, subtler flavor.) When the ginger is cool, mince it finely.

2. In a medium-sized mixing bowl, add all the other ingredients to the ginger, except the oil and salt and pepper, and mix well.

3. While mixing constantly, slowly add the oil in a steady stream. Add salt and pepper to taste. Will keep, covered and refrigerated, for about 1 week.

ABOUT 1 PINT

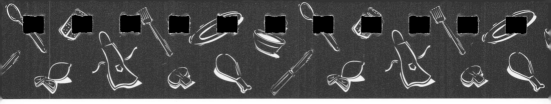

HOMEMADE MAYONNAISE (WITH VARIATIONS)

Mayonnaises are great for grilled fish because the velvety texture and plain flavor of the basic mayonnaise provides a subtle vehicle for spicy flavorings. An example of this is the chipotle mayonnaise, which is an excellent partner for the strong-charactered grilled bluefish. To make the variations, just mix the ingredients into the basic mayonnaise until well blended. The mayonnaises will keep 4 to 5 weeks, covered and refrigerated.

Yolks of 2 large eggs
1 tablespoon lemon juice (about ¼ lemon)
½ teaspoon salt
½ teaspoon freshly ground pepper (white is best if you have it)
1 teaspoon prepared brown mustard
1 cup vegetable oil

1. Blend the egg yolks and lemon juice in a food processor or blender for 30 seconds.

2. With the machine still running, add the salt, pepper, and mustard, and continue to blend for an additional 30 seconds.

3. With the machine still running, slowly add the oil in a steady stream until it is completely emulsified with the egg yolk mixture.

ABOUT 1 CUP

TEXAS PETE MAYONNAISE

This is the result of my attempt to recreate a mayonnaise I had while on vacation on the Outer Banks of North Carolina, where it was served with a fried fish platter in a small seafood restaurant. The only information I could get out of the chef about this mayo was something to the effect

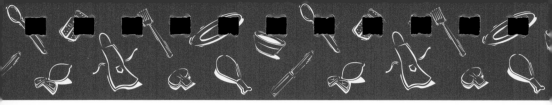

that he put in "a bottle of Texas Pete," a local hot sauce. I made my own variation when I got back home, and it is in fact very similar to the one I had back at the fish shack on the beach.

1 cup basic mayonnaise
1 teaspoon cayenne pepper
2 tablespoons ketchup
1 tablespoon chili powder
2 dashes of Worcestershire sauce

ABOUT 1 CUP

CHIPOTLE PEPPER MAYONNAISE

This variation needs a major strong flavor to go up against. The chipotles, which are smoked jalapeño peppers, add a nice bit of fire to this mayo.

1 cup basic mayonnaise
1 tablespoon minced canned chipotles (see Pantry)
1 teaspoon minced garlic

1 tablespoon tomato purée
2 tablespoons lime juice (about 1 lime)
2 tablespoons chopped cilantro
Salt and freshly cracked black pepper to taste

ABOUT 1 CUP

SARDINE AND CAPER MAYONNAISE

1 cup basic mayonnaise
6 sardines, coarsely chopped
2 tablespoons capers
1 tablespoon lemon juice (about ¼ lemon)
Dash of cayenne
2 tablespoons chopped parsley

1. Chop sardines roughly. In a medium bowl, mix the sardines with all other ingredients.

2. Add to one cup mayonnaise. Mix well. Keeps 4 to 5 days, covered and refrigerated.

ABOUT 1 CUP

COMPOUND BUTTERS

◆

Compound butters are a quick, easy way to add a little dash to grilled fish but still let the fish be the focus. They are easy to make and you can roll them into tubes, cover them with plastic wrap, put them in the freezer, and then just cut slices the size you need. A small pat on top of your fish or chicken will melt and spread its flavor over the food. Don't forget that herb butters are a good way to use those remaining fresh herbs when the first frost is coming.

Here are some ideas to use as general guidelines for creating your own compound butters. All are added to 1 pound of very soft unsalted butter, then blended thoroughly in a food processor or by hand if necessary.

BASIL-LEMON

4 tablespoons chopped basil
4 tablespoons lemon juice (about 1 lemon)
1 tablespoon minced garlic
Salt and freshly cracked black pepper to taste

ROSEMARY-GARLIC-BLACK PEPPER

3 tablespoons rosemary needles
1 tablespoon minced garlic
2 tablespoons freshly cracked black pepper
Salt to taste

GINGER-SCALLION

4 tablespoons scallion
2 tablespoons minced fresh ginger
1 tablespoon rice wine vinegar
Salt and freshly cracked black pepper to taste

HONEY-SAGE RAISIN

3 tablespoons chopped fresh sage
4 tablespoons honey
¼ cup raisins
Salt and freshly cracked black pepper to taste

HOT CHILE-CILANTRO

4 tablespoons chopped cilantro
2 tablespoons minced fresh red serrano chile
  peppers
2 tablespoons lime juice (about 1 lime)
Salt and freshly cracked black pepper to taste

CHILE

3 tablespoons chili powder
1 tablespoon ground cumin
3 dashes of Tabasco sauce
2 tablespoons tequila
Salt and freshly cracked black pepper to taste

SESAME

4 tablespoons sesame seeds, roasted in a single
  layer in a 350°F oven for 25 minutes
2 tablespoons sesame oil
2 tablespoons chopped scallion

BALSAMIC, BASIL, AND BLACK PEPPER MUSTARD

Mustards using freshly ground seeds may seem semitoxic on the first whiff, so you need to let them air out for a while. These guys are very potent and my recommendation is that they be used in conjunction with some bread and meat, as I think their power would dominate fish or even chicken. I especially like these with tenderloin sandwiches or any leftover grilled red meat.

⅓ cup dark mustard seeds
4 tablespoons water
2 tablespoons balsamic vinegar
1 tablespoon dry mustard
2 tablespoons honey
1 teaspoon freshly cracked black pepper
2 tablespoons chopped fresh basil
Salt to taste

1. Grind the mustard seeds in a spice blender or with a mortar and pestle until they have become a fine powder. Place the powder in a bowl.

2. Add the water and vinegar, stir well, and allow the mixture to stand for 1 to 2 hours.

3. Add all the remaining ingredients and blend well. This mixture will keep, covered and refrigerated, up to 4 months.

ABOUT 1 CUP

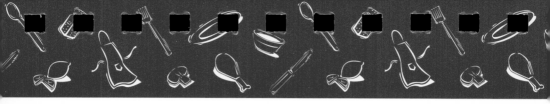

THAI-STYLE ALL-PURPOSE HOT MIXED CURRY PASTE

In Thailand, there is an almost infinite variety of curries served in every possible manner. Here I have made a very bold curry paste, one whose flavor will stand out when it is used with grilled foods. Keep this paste in the refrigerator and use it as a flavor enhancer. It may be substituted in any recipe that calls for powdered curry and will give you more depth of flavor. Put a couple of teaspoons in your barbecue sauce for an added whoop. Or try diluting it with a little butter and brushing it over thin pork chops before you grill them.

2 fresh green chile peppers
3 tablespoons minced fresh lemongrass (see Pantry) or 2 teaspoons dried
1 tablespoon minced garlic
2 tablespoons chopped fresh ginger
1 teaspoon grated lime zest (green part only)
1 tablespoon red pepper flakes
2 tablespoons ground coriander seed
2 tablespoons ground cumin
1 teaspoon ground cardamom
1 teaspoon cinnamon
1 tablespoon freshly cracked pepper (white is best if you have it)
1 teaspoon salt

Put all the ingredients together in a blender or food processor and purée into a paste. That's all, folks! Keeps, covered and refrigerated, for up to 6 weeks.

ABOUT 1 CUP

ALL THE FIXIN'S

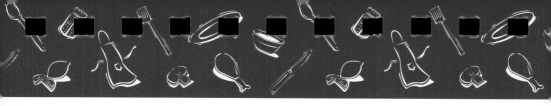

MARINATED FETA WITH ROASTED RED PEPPERS, BLACK OLIVES, AND THYME

This southern Mediterranean combination is a fantastic addition to a large summer buffet. Its richness goes well with grilled meat and can be enjoyed by itself or with salads like Grilled Eggplant with Olive Oil, Parsley, and Capers (recipe 90).

1 pound feta cheese, diced large (about 16 pieces)
1 cup fresh black Greek olives, pitted
2 roasted red bell peppers (see Pantry)
½ cup extra virgin olive oil
1 small red onion, diced small
1 teaspoon minced garlic
1 tablespoon red wine vinegar
2 tablespoons fresh thyme
Salt and freshly cracked black pepper to taste
8 tablespoons lemon juice (about 2 lemons)

1. In a large bowl, combine the feta, olives, and red peppers. Add the olive oil and toss lightly.

2. Add the onion, garlic, vinegar, thyme, salt and pepper, and toss again.

3. Squeeze the lemon juice over the mixture, and allow it to stand 2 to 3 hours in the refrigerator before serving. Will keep, covered and refrigerated, about 4 days.

SERVES 6 AS AN ANTIPASTO

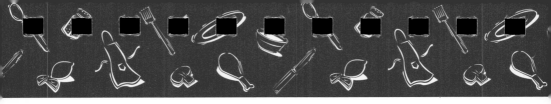

JOSÉ'S JICAMA SLAW

To me, "slaw" means an assortment of inexpensive fresh vegetables thinly sliced or grated and combined with a dressing. Cabbage is obviously the classic, but slaw can feature many other vegetables. In this case, the jicama and West Indies-slanted seasonings combine to create a new wave, island version with a slightly exotic flavor and crunchy texture—another dish created by my day chef, José Velasquez, who has the uncanny ability to make anything taste good. This is an easy dish to prepare for large groups—it's no more difficult than your basic coleslaw.

5 cups grated green cabbage
2 cups grated carrot
2 cups peeled and julienned jicama

FOR THE DRESSING
1 cup chopped cilantro
½ cup cheap yellow mustard
½ cup ketchup
4 tablespoons white vinegar
2 teaspoons sugar
1 garlic clove, minced
Salt and freshly cracked black pepper to taste

1. Place the cabbage, grated carrot, and jicama in a large bowl.

2. In a food processor or blender, mix all the dressing ingredients until well integrated. Pour this over the vegetables, and mix well.

SERVES 8 TO 10 AS A SIDE DISH

SERVING SUGGESTIONS: Serve this with traditional barbecued meats or any grilled red meat, such as Grilled Lime-Marinated Flank Steak with Chipotle-Honey Sauce (recipe 46).

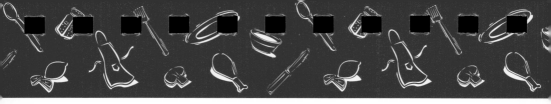

GRILLED EGGPLANT WITH OLIVE OIL, PARSLEY, AND CAPERS

◆

Eggplant on the grill is a natural. It's straightforward, easy, and goes well as a vegetable with grilled chicken or fish. A lot of people would advise you to salt the eggplant before grilling to remove the bitterness, but I find that if the eggplant is grilled immediately after cutting, that is not necessary.

This dish adapts itself well to advance preparation. If you want to, you can grill the eggplant and refrigerate it, covered, up to 3 days, then at the last minute julienne it, mix all the ingredients together, and add a touch of red wine.

2 large eggplants
¾ cup extra virgin olive oil
Salt and freshly cracked black pepper to taste
½ cup chopped parsley
4 tablespoons capers
8 tablespoons lemon juice (about 2 lemons)

1. Just before grilling, slice the eggplants into ½-inch-thick slices. Brush with a bit of the olive oil and season with salt and pepper to taste.

2. Over medium heat, grill the eggplant slices on one side until golden dark brown, about 3 to 4 minutes. Turn them and grill the other side in the same manner.

3. Remove the eggplant slices to a platter large enough to lay them out in a single layer. Pour the remaining olive oil over the slices, sprinkle them with the parsley and capers, and squeeze the lemon juice over them. Serve at once.

SERVES 6 AS A SIDE DISH

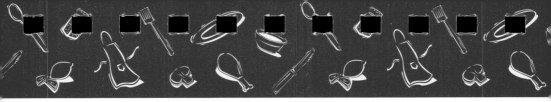

WEST INDIES BREADFRUIT SALAD

◆

Breadfruit comes from the West Indies. It is a starchy vegetable and is used like a potato. It can be fried, baked, or boiled. This is a dish to make when you are tired of getting that same ole potato salad.

1 3- to 4-pound breadfruit (see Pantry)
1 cup chopped celery
1 large red onion, diced small
4 fresh red or green jalapeño chile peppers, finely chopped

FOR THE DRESSING
1 ripe mango, peeled, pitted, and puréed
4 tablespoons cider vinegar
2 tablespoons dark rum
8 tablespoons lime juice (about 4 limes)
1½ cups mayonnaise
4 tablespoons chopped cilantro
2 tablespoons minced fresh ginger
Salt and freshly cracked black pepper to taste

1. Prepare the breadfruit: Peel and slice it in half, then remove the center core and cut the fruit into bite-size cubes. Cook them in boiling water to cover for 10 to 15 minutes, until easily pierced with a fork. Remove them from the heat, drain, and cool to room temperature.

2. Place the room-temperature breadfruit in a mixing bowl. Add the celery, onion, and jalapeño, and mix lightly. Make the dressing: Whisk the mango purée, cider vinegar, rum, and lime juice into the mayonnaise. Blend in the cilantro and ginger. Season with salt and pepper to taste.

3. Fold the dressing into the breadfruit and serve. Will keep, covered and refrigerated, 4 days.

SERVES 6 AS A SIDE DISH

SERVING SUGGESTIONS: Serve with Grilled Jamaican Jerk Chicken with Banana-Guava Ketchup (recipe 56).

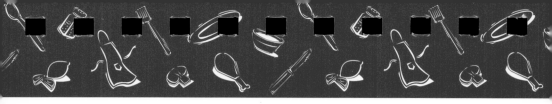

SWEET POTATO HASH BROWNS WITH BACON AND ONIONS

Using sweet potatoes makes this a richer dish than traditional hash browns.

4 medium sweet potatoes (about 2 pounds), peeled
6 slices bacon, diced
1 large yellow onion, sliced
½ cup peanut oil
Salt and freshly cracked black pepper to taste
4 tablespoons chopped parsley

1. Place the potatoes in a saucepan with cold water to cover. Bring them to a boil and cook until a skewer can start to go through them easily, 15 to 20 minutes. If you are unsure, it is better to undercook a bit rather than overcook in this situation.

2. Remove the potatoes from the heat, drain, and cover with cold water. Allow the potatoes to cool to room temperature, then cut them into chunks the size of large dice.

3. In a large sauté pan over medium heat, cook the bacon pieces until nearly done (just starting to crisp up). Add the onion and cook both until the onion is colored gold to brown, about 7 minutes. Remove both from the sauté pan and reserve.

4. Wipe the sauté pan and return it to the stove over medium-high heat. Add the peanut oil, and heat it until very hot but not smoking. Test by tossing a chunk of potato in—you should see some action, Jackson.

5. Put the potato chunks in the oil and panfry them until golden brown, about 7 to 8 minutes, turning occasionally. Watch out for the splattering oil.

6. Remove the pan from the heat, add the bacon and onion, season with salt and pepper to taste, and sprinkle with parsley.

SERVES 6 AS A SIDE DISH

SWEET POTATO SALAD

◆

A new variation on an old theme. I use sweet potatoes instead of the blander white potatoes and dress them with a light vinaigrette. I like it better than mayonnaise, and the resulting salad is a little more versatile.

4 medium sweet potatoes (about 2 pounds),
   peeled and cut into uniform large pieces
½ red bell pepper, seeded and diced small
½ green bell pepper, seeded and diced small
½ large red onion, diced small
4 tablespoons finely chopped parsley

FOR THE DRESSING
3 tablespoons Dijon mustard
3 tablespoons ketchup
1 teaspoon minced garlic
¾ cup olive oil
4 tablespoons cider vinegar
1 tablespoon Worcestershire sauce
2 tablespoons lime juice (about 1 lime)
Salt and freshly cracked black pepper to taste

1. Plug up your sink and fill it with about 5 quarts of cold water and a couple of trays of ice cubes.

2. In 3 quarts of boiling salted water, cook the pieces of sweet potato until just done, 10 to 12 minutes. Be careful not to overcook. You should be able to pierce them with a fork, but you should still feel some resistance, and the pieces should not fall apart.

3. Remove the pieces of sweet potato from the heat, drain, and immediately plunge them into the ice-water bath. After 30 seconds, drain them again, and put them into a large stainless steel bowl. Add the diced pepper, onion, and parsley.

4. Make the dressing: Place the mustard, ketchup, and garlic in a medium-sized bowl. Whisking constantly, add the olive oil in a slow, steady stream. Add the vinegar, Worcestershire sauce, and lime juice, and mix well. Season with salt and pepper to taste.

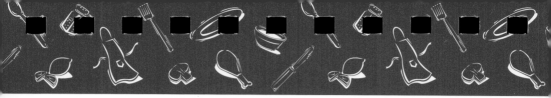

5. Pour the dressing over the sweet potato mixture, and toss gently. Serve immediately, or it will keep, covered and refrigerated, for up to 5 days.

SERVES 6 AS A SIDE DISH

SERVING SUGGESTIONS: This salad goes with just about anything. Try it with Grilled Pork Birdies with Tangerine Rosemary Glaze (recipe 53) or Soy-Marinated Scallops with Grilled Shiitakes (recipe 39).

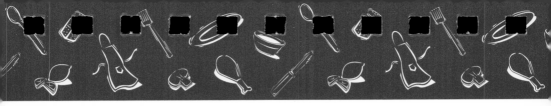

DOC'S CHEDDAR BISCUITS

Another Southern tradition that has been imported to the North for my annual Christmas party, where I serve these with Grilled Country Ham and Applesauce (recipe 44), along with a heavily spiked eggnog. These little guys are also known in the South as "ham biscuits" and are so popular that they have almost become a generic term for hors d'oeuvres, as in "Don't y'all fill up on them ham biscuits, darlin'."

5 cups all-purpose flour
2 tablespoons baking powder
4 tablespoons sugar
½ teaspoon salt
1 cup heavy cream
1 cup buttermilk
½ pound (16 tablespoons) butter, melted
1 cup grated cheddar cheese

1. Preheat the oven to 350°F.

2. Sift together the flour, baking powder, sugar, and salt.

3. If you have a paddle attachment on your mixer, use it at low speed to mix the heavy cream, buttermilk, and three fourths (12 tablespoons) of the melted butter in with the sifted ingredients. Otherwise, use a wooden spoon for mixing. In either case, mix only until the dough just pulls together, but is still somewhat crumbly.

4. Turn the dough out onto a floured surface and finish incorporating the dry ingredients by hand with a gentle kneading motion. Do not overwork the dough.

5. Form the dough into a rectangular shape, and using a rolling pin on a floured surface, roll the dough out to ½-inch thickness, keeping the edges as square as possible. Brush half of the rectangle with the remaining melted butter (4 tablespoons), and sprinkle the cheese over this

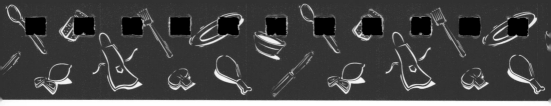

half. Using the edge of your hand, make an indentation at the middle of the dough (just give it a good karate chop), then fold the unbuttered half over the cheese-covered half. Press down evenly with your hands.

6. Using a rolling pin, roll the dough (which should now be about 1 inch thick) down to ¾-inch thickness. Wrap the dough in waxed paper, and chill for about ½ hour to firm it up.

7. When the dough is chilled, with a biscuit or round cookie cutter, cut rounds from the dough, place them on an ungreased baking sheet, and bake for 40 minutes, or until the tops are golden brown. The biscuits should split at the center during baking, exposing the cheese and making a handy configuration for a nice ham sandwich.

1 DOZEN

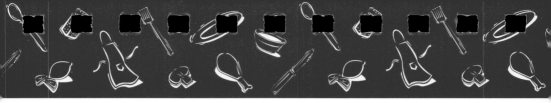

YOUR BASIC BLACK BEANS

◆

A staple in much of the world. Cook a big batch and keep it in the refrigerator to heat up anytime you need 'em. These are good by themselves or with rice, providing a smooth, comforting complement to spicy grilled foods. The beer gives a touch of malty flavor. I prefer a dark or amber beer, but use what you like.

2 cups dried black beans
2 large yellow onions, diced small
4 tablespoons peanut oil
2 tablespoons minced garlic
1 teaspoon chili powder
1 teaspoon ground cumin
1 teaspoon Tabasco sauce
1 teaspoon sugar
4 tablespoons white vinegar
2 cups water
1 bottle of your favorite beer
Salt and freshly cracked black pepper to taste
3 scallions, chopped, for garnish

1. Soak the beans in cold water to cover for 5 hours, then drain and rinse them well.

2. In a saucepan, sauté the onion in the peanut oil over medium-high heat until clear, 4 to 5 minutes.

3. Add the garlic, and cook another minute.

4. Add the chili powder, cumin, Tabasco sauce, sugar, vinegar, water, and beer, and bring to a simmer.

5. Add the beans, bring everything to a simmer again, then cover well and cook over low heat for 3 hours or until the beans are soft to the bite. If you think additional liquid is needed, add more beer.

6. Finish the dish by seasoning with salt and pepper to taste, and garnish with chopped scallion. Keeps up to 1 week, covered and refrigerated.

SERVES 6 TO 8 AS A SIDE DISH

BLACK BEAN SALAD

This dish is Mexican/Southwestern in concept. It's a bit like a salad of greens, where black beans substitute for the lettuce and the rather large dose of lime juice makes it surprisingly refreshing. It travels well and is better the day after it's made; a good accompaniment to hot or cold grilled meat. You can also add cold grilled meat to the salad and turn it into an entrée.

FOR THE BEANS
1 pound dried black turtle beans
½ teaspoon dried thyme
½ teaspoon salt
¼ teaspoon fennel seed
2 fat garlic cloves, peeled
1 bay leaf

FOR THE DRESSING
⅔ cup chopped red onion
½ cup chopped red bell pepper
2 tablespoons chopped parsley
2 tablespoons chopped cilantro
2 tablespoons chopped scallion
1 tablespoon ground cumin

⅛ teaspoon cayenne pepper
4 tablespoons olive oil
10 tablespoons lime juice (about 5 limes)
Salt and freshly cracked black pepper to taste

1. Sort the beans carefully, discarding any small pebbles that may be mixed in. Soak the beans in cold water to cover for 5 hours, then drain and rinse them well.

2. Put the beans in a saucepan and add enough water to come about 1½ inches above them.

3. Add the thyme, salt, fennel seed, garlic, and bay leaf. Bring to a boil, then reduce the heat and simmer, uncovered, for 1 to 1½ hours, or until the beans are tender but not mushy.

4. Drain the beans and rinse them under cold water for 1 minute to stop the cooking process. Drain them again.

5. In a large bowl, combine the dressing ingredients and mix well. Add the beans, toss, and serve. This salad keeps for 4 to 5 days, covered and refrigerated.

SERVES 6 TO 8

YOUR BASIC GRILLED CORN

◆

There are any number of methods for dealing with corn on the grill, each with its own merits. After many years of experimentation, I have settled on the following method, which is a combination of several techniques.

The traditional method has you peel away the outer husk without actually removing it, remove the inner silky threads, then wrap the outer husk back around the ear. You then soak the ear in water and finally place it on the grill, where it cooks by steaming. This method produces tasty corn, but to me it is missing the taste of the fire. So I follow this method until the corn is just cooked, which takes about 15 to 20 minutes over a low fire. I then remove the husks, brush on a little butter, season with salt and pepper, and roll the ears around on the grill ever so slightly, just to add a little char.

Another method calls for the interior silk to be removed and for the corn to then be wrapped in foil along with butter and seasonings and roasted in the coals for 12 to 15 minutes. This is also an excellent method, although again it misses the taste of the fire.

Whichever technique you use, summer corn cooked on the grill is a welcome addition to any meal, its natural simplicity making for some outstanding eating.

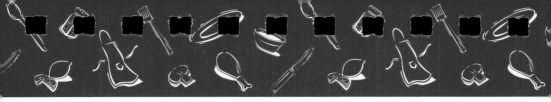

PICKLED CHILE PEPPERS

◆

If you find chile peppers you really like, or if you simply have an abundance from your garden, you might want to consider pickling them. There will be a slight change in their flavor, but the heat and their general characteristics will remain the same.

Make enough pickling solution to cover the amount of chile peppers that you have, mixing the ingredients in the following proportions:

*1 cup vinegar to ½ cup sugar to 2 cloves of
    garlic*

Bring this mixture to a boil over high heat, remove it from the heat, pour it over the chile peppers to cover, and cool to room temperature. Put in a jar with a tight cover, making sure that the liquid completely covers the peppers. They will keep this way for up to 3 months at room temperature.

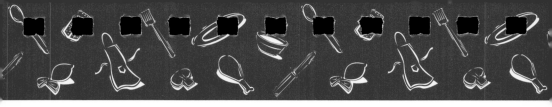

GRANDMA WETZLER'S BAKED BEANS

◆

Made from my grandma's Pennsylvania Dutch recipe, these beans just can't be beat. Filling, satisfying, and slightly sweet, no picnic or barbecue feast is complete without them.

½ pound bacon, diced
1 yellow onion, diced small
1 gallon water
½ cup molasses
½ cup brown sugar
2 cups ketchup
2 tablespoons cheap yellow mustard
1¼ pounds navy beans (soaked in water to
    cover overnight)
Salt and freshly cracked black pepper to taste

1. In a large pot, sauté the bacon over medium heat until browned, about 5 minutes.

2. Add the diced onions and cook until browned, about 5 minutes.

3. Add the water, molasses, brown sugar, ketchup, and mustard, and bring to a boil.

4. Add the beans, bring back up to a boil, then reduce to a slow simmer and cook 4 to 5 hours until the beans are soft, adding water from time to time if necessary and stirring often to prevent burning. Season with salt and pepper to taste. These beans will keep, covered and refrigerated, about 1 week.

SERVES 10 AS A SIDE DISH

SERVING SUGGESTIONS: Serve these with any picnic food or barbecue.

EAST COAST GRILL CORN BREAD

◆

This is an ubiquitous companion to Southwestern and Southern dishes. It is perfect for mopping up pot likker or cooling off your palate after hot dishes. If you have any left over, cut it into small cubes and bake them in a 350°F oven for 30 to 45 minutes, until brown and toasty, and you have marvelous croutons for your green salads.

4 cups all-purpose flour
2 cups yellow cornmeal
1½ cups sugar
1 teaspoon salt
2 tablespoons baking powder
4 eggs
3 cups milk
2½ tablespoons vegetable oil
½ cup melted butter

1. Preheat the oven to 350°F.
2. Lightly oil a 2"x 12"x 8" pan.

3. Sift together the flour, cornmeal, sugar, salt, and baking powder.

4. In a separate bowl, mix together the eggs, milk, and vegetable oil.

5. Pour the wet ingredients over the dry ingredients, then add the melted butter. Stir until just mixed.

6. Bake for approximately 1 hour, or until a cake tester comes out clean. The corn bread should be brown when done.

12 THICK PIECES

PANTRY

◆

PANTRY OF PROCESSES

TO BRAISE GARLIC:

A head of garlic will yield about 4 tablespoons (2 ounces) of braised garlic. To prepare it, place the whole, unpeeled head of garlic in the center of a foot-long sheet of tinfoil, pour about 3 tablespoons of virgin olive oil over the entire bulb of garlic, and wrap it up very tightly. Roast in a 300°F oven for about 1 hour, or until the individual garlic cloves are soft to the touch. Remove the bulb from the oven and allow it to cool to room temperature, which will take about ½ hour. If necessary, you can refrigerate the bulb at this point and remove the pulp later, but it is much easier to do while the cloves are still warm. In either case, be sure you reserve the oil in which the garlic has roasted.

To remove the pulp, simply break the individual cloves of garlic from the bulb and squeeze out the inner meat. (There is no need to cut open each clove, since it will break when you separate it from the bulb.) When all the cloves have been squeezed, add the reserved oil to the meat. The oil has a deep garlic flavor and will prolong the shelf life of the braised garlic. With the oil, braised garlic can be stored, covered and refrigerated, about 2 weeks; without the oil it lasts only 1 week.

TO ROAST RED BELL PEPPERS:

Roasting a bell pepper removes the skin and adds a rich, smoky flavor. It might seem like an odd technique the first time you do it, but sprinkle the resulting peppers with salt and pepper and a little olive oil, splash them with balsamic vinegar, and you'll be torching these babies every time the grill is out.

With the fire at high heat, take 5 red bell peppers and whip them on the grill. Now, I know that this goes against your better instincts, but you're going to burn them until they are completely black. It is theoretically possible to burn them too much, but if you kind of roll them around until they are completely dark and the skin is well blistered, you've got it right. Remove the peppers from the grill, pop them into a brown paper bag, tie

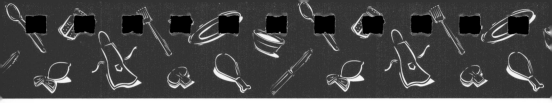

the bag shut, and allow the peppers to cool in the bag for 1 hour. This facilitates the removal of the burned skins.

After 1 hour, remove the peppers from the bag and sort of fondle them in your hands, caressing the skins into falling off. Tear the peppers in half, remove the inner cores and seeds, and run the peppers gently under cold water to remove any remaining charred pieces of skin. That's it. Put them in a small container, cover with olive oil, cover the container, and refrigerate. They will keep up to 2 weeks stored in this manner. If you wish, a fresh herb such as basil or rosemary and a little chopped garlic can be added to complement the flavor of the peppers.

TO MAKE COCONUT MILK:

Do not confuse this staple of Indonesian cooking with the liquid in the center of a coconut, often mistakenly referred to by the same name. The following procedure will yield about 2 cups of milk.

Remove the outer husk of a 1½-pound coconut by throwing it repeatedly at a brick wall or the sidewalk—or you can smash it with a hammer. This should render the coconut into 4 to 6 smaller, more manageable pieces. With a blunt object such as a potato peeler, pry off the outer husk from each piece. The thinner brown inner skin can be left on. Put the husked coconut pieces into a food processor or blender and purée until it is very fine, with no large chunks. Turn off the food processor or blender, add 2 cups of boiling water, then blend for about 10 seconds. Remove the mixture from the food processor or blender and strain it through a fine sieve or cheesecloth. Reserve the liquid (the "milk") and discard the solids. The milk will keep in the refrigerator, covered, up to 10 days.

If you live near an Asian, Indian, or Caribbean market, you will be able to find canned coconut milk, which is a good product. Do not confuse this with Coco Lopez, a sweetened coconut-flavored cream.

PANTRY OF PRODUCTS

ACHIOTE: The Spanish name for the seed from a small tropical tree. It is used in Latin America primarily to color lard, either in seed form or ground up and made into a paste. It does not have a very pronounced flavor and paprika is an acceptable substitute.

CHIPOTLES: Dried, smoked jalapeño pep-

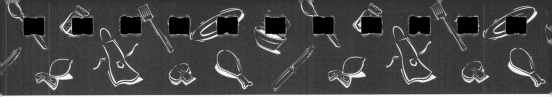

pers, available dried or canned. I prefer canned. If chipotles are unavailable, you may substitute a mixture of Liquid Smoke, 2 to 3 puréed fresh chile peppers of your choice, and 3 tablespoons ketchup.

GUAVA PASTE: This Brazilian product has a supersweet concentrated guava taste and is found in 1-pound cans in Latin markets.

HOISIN: A Chinese sauce made from soy sauce, yellow beans, sugar, vinegar, and spices, hoisin is used both in conjunction with other sauces and by itself. It is found in all Asian markets and some supermarkets in cans and jars.

KOSHER SALT: This coarse-grained sea salt containing natural iodine is the only type that I use.

MISO (AKA FERMENTED BEAN PASTE): This Japanese staple is the result of injecting mold into boiled soybeans. The addition of wheat, rice, or barley produces varying strengths, colors, and flavors. In Japanese cooking, miso is used in everything from salad dressings to soup to condiments for grilled foods, and its versatility and adaptability make it a wonderful item with which to experiment.

OILS: You should keep at least three types of oil handy. First, an inexpensive vegetable oil to coat foods before grilling. There's no point in using a better or tastier oil, since the flavor is lost during grilling anyway, and the oil is used only to prevent sticking. Second, a low- to medium-quality olive oil for use in relishes and dressings. The taste of the oil does come through somewhat in these preparations, but it is usually dominated by the other ingredients. Finally, a very fine, expensive, extra virgin olive oil. I break this out only for those dishes in which the olive oil is really going to stand out—those late-summer tomatoes eaten with basil, salt, pepper, and a drizzle of olive oil, for example, or Grilled Pompano with Lime and Olive Oil (recipe 25).

PEPPER, FRESHLY CRACKED, BLACK OR WHITE: Pepper is used in almost every recipe in this book, and I can't emphasize strongly enough how important it is that you use freshly cracked. It has a strong impact on a dish.

You can either use a pepper mill or place the peppercorns on a cutting board or other

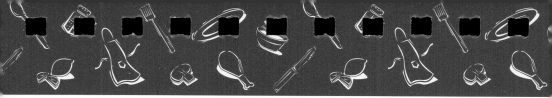

over them. If you use a mill, though, I recommend that you set it to its coarsest grind.

In many of my seafood and Asian-inspired recipes, I suggest using white pepper. This is because I find the more aromatic, less robust nature of this pepper to be more appropriate for these rather delicate dishes.

PICKLED GINGER (AKA *GARI*):
A traditional Japanese raw fish accompaniment, this very thinly sliced, vinegared ginger has a natural affinity for grilled food. It is available in Japanese markets or in the Japanese sections of Asian markets. It will keep indefinitely in your refrigerator, covered, in its liquid.

SESAME OIL:
Made from sesame seeds, this oil has a very pronounced, nutty/ burned flavor and is used more for flavoring than for straight cooking.

TOMATILLO:
This Latin American staple looks like a small, unripe tomato with a brown husk. It is cooked and used in sauces and salsas in Latin cuisines, and is widely available canned as well as fresh.

VINEGARS:
Vinegars, along with citrus juices, are high-acid liquids that stimulate the sour taste buds on the tongue. As such, they are excellent flavor balancers, helping to bring other strong tastes into harmony. I use many kinds in my recipes—red wine, cider, white, rice wine, and balsamic. Rice wine vinegar is a beautifully delicate vinegar, its subtle sweetness being its major characteristic. My personal favorite, however, is the balsamic vinegar of Italy. A sprinkle will bring a simple piece of grilled meat or poultry to life, drawing out its innate flavor.

WASABI (AKA JAPANESE HORSE-RADISH):
A traditional Japanese accompaniment to raw fish, this root is more aromatic but less powerful than the white root we know as horseradish. In the United States it is available as a paste or as powder that you mix with water yourself to form a paste. I find the powder to be far superior than the premade paste.

PANTRY OF PRODUCE

BONIATO (AKA BATATA OR CUBAN SWEET POTATO):
This is basically a white sweet potato. Originally a New World product, it is widely used in Asia as well as in

the Caribbean and South America. In the United States, it is found mostly in Latin markets.

BREADFRUIT: Breadfruit grows on almost every Caribbean island and also on the mainland of South America as far south as Brazil.

The breadfruit tree is a prolific producer of its fruit, which is actually a vegetable. As with a number of other tropical fruits and vegetables, it is eaten in its green, ripe, and overripe stages. The flesh is fibrous but is prepared in the same manner as a potato. Breadfruit is sold all year long in West Indian markets.

JICAMA: This tuber has a taste that lies somewhere between an apple and a potato. Its crunchy texture and slightly sweet taste have become increasingly familiar here as part of the Southwestern food trend. Peel its skin off with a knife, cover it with water, and jicama will keep covered in the refrigerator for up to 2 days. Jicama can be found in Latin and Asian markets and some supermarkets.

LEMONGRASS: It is this grass, grown in tropical areas around the world, that produces the characteristic flavor of Thai and Vietnamese cuisines. The inedible, tough upper stems are excellent for infusing stocks and soups and are used in many parts of the world to make tea, while the bottom section can be chopped fine and used directly in recipes. To prepare lemongrass, remove the stems above the bottom third (the bulb) and reserve them for use in broths, soups, or teas. Remove the outer leaves from the bottom third, and inside you will find a tender core. Mince this core very fine as you would ginger or garlic, and add to dishes as directed. It is found in Asian and specialty markets. Although not as aromatic, dried lemongrass makes a decent substitute.

MALANGA (AKA YAUTIA): This Caribbean root vegetable is very similar in appearance to the taro of the Pacific. Mealy and starchy, it has a more dynamic flavor than its many brother tubers, its distinct earthy flavor hinting of beans or nuts. Like many other tubers, it is prepared in the same way as potatoes. Available in West Indian markets.

MANGO: Along with the watermelon, this is one of my very favorite fruits. Like the papaya, the mango is used in its green state as a veg-

etable, either cooked or added raw to salads. The flesh is somewhat difficult to get at, but well worth the effort, since the person who does the job gets to suck and gnaw on the pit. In urban areas, mangoes are sold in Asian markets and even many supermarkets.

PAPAYA: Used as both a fruit and a vegetable, the papaya is native to the Caribbean and is found in tropical regions throughout the world. It can grow up to twenty pounds in size. The musky-flavored fruit—also known for its ability to tenderize meat—ranges in color from greenish-yellow when underripe to bright orange and in some cases even red when fully ripe. It is used as a salad ingredient, cooked in soups, or eaten raw as a kind of snack food with just a squeeze of lime juice. Unfortunately, this fruit travels poorly, so most Americans have never had the opportunity to taste it at its peak. In urban areas, papayas are sold in Latin markets, specialty stores, and some supermarkets.

PLANTAIN (AKA GREEN BANANA, COOKING BANANA): This tropical relative of the banana is always cooked before being eaten. In its green state, it has the starchy qual-

ity of a potato, but by the time it is ripe (the skin will be black), the starch has turned to sugar. In its ripe stage, the plantain is used in desserts or as snack food. Popular in the West Indies, Central America, Africa, and Asia, it keeps for a long time and is a wonderfully adaptable ingredient with which to experiment in stews, fritters, and desserts. In urban areas, plantains are found in Latin and West Indian markets.

TAMARIND: This fruit consists of a pod from 3 to 6 inches long covered with brown, furry skin, and containing sweetish dark brown pulp along with several seeds. It is used to flavor a number of condiments, of which Worcestershire sauce is the most familiar to Americans. In Latin cuisines, its tart flavor is sometimes substituted for lemon or lime. It is sold in a convenient-to-use paste form in Asian and Indian markets.

YUCA (AKA CASSAVA OR MANIOC): This sticky, bland root vegetable is widely used in Africa as well as Central and South America, and in the South Pacific it is combined with coconuts to make desserts. The yuca is generally prepared in the same way as a

yuca is generally prepared in the same way as a potato, except that it contains a main central fiber which must be removed before cooking. It is available in Latin markets.

PEPPERS AND CHILES

Peppers vary widely in heat, so you can decide for yourself just how much of a thrill you want.

Let me give you a brief description of each of the chile peppers used in this book, progressing from mild to mind-blowing.

ANCHO: A dried chile, this pepper has more flavor than heat. To prepare one (or more) for use in cooking, remove the seeds, toast it lightly, then place it in a bowl, add boiling water to cover, and allow it to soak for 40 minutes. Physical description: Flat, dark brown to red; 2 to 3 inches long and about 1½ inches wide.

ROCOTILLO: One of the few peppers for which I feel there is no substitute. It has all the aromaticity and flavor of the awesome Scotch Bonnet (*habañero*) with none of its heat. The fascinating rocotillo can be found in West Indian and Latin markets, but be careful—while smaller in size, it is similar in shape to the king of heat, the Scotch Bonnet. Physical description: Shaped like a wrinkled pattypan squash; red, orange, or various shades of green; very small, like a bottle cap.

CHIPOTLE: A dried, smoked jalapeño, it usually comes canned, packed in a tomato sauce. If you find dried ones, they can be reconstituted by soaking in boiling water for 40 minutes. Their strong, imposing flavor makes them my favorite dried chile. A little goes a long way, since their smoky, earthy heat is strong and forceful. I use chipotles not only in sauces and relishes, but also in salad dressings, mayonnaises, and butters. Physical description: Flat and wrinkled; dark reddish-brown; 1 to 1½ inches long.

JALAPEÑO: Probably the largest cash chile pepper crop, this is the most widely known pepper in the United States. It is easy to find and, although relatively low on the heat scale, it still packs a decent punch. Although the red variety is a bit more difficult to find than the green, I find it has a richer flavor. Physical description: Plump and bullet-shaped; either red or green, with a sleek and shiny look;

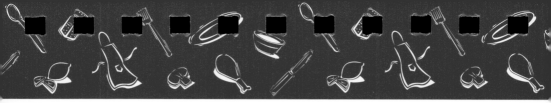

about 1 to 1½ inches long.

SERRANO: Like the jalapeño, the serrano is native to Mexico, but it is less widely available in the United States. These "green bullets from hell" are one step up the heat ladder from jalapeños. Physical description: Shaped like a skinny jalapeño, either red or green; 1 to 1½ inches long and ½ inch in diameter.

TABASCO: A step hotter yet, this chile pepper was popularized by the McIlhenney Company of Louisiana in the hot sauce that bears the pepper's name. The sauce itself makes a good heat source. Physical description: Shaped like a blunt jalapeño with wrinkled skin; red, yellow, or orange; 1 to 1½ inches long.

CAYENNE: Turn it up one more notch. This chile pepper, found all over the world, is most familiar to us in its powdered form but can also be found fresh. Either is fine. The Chile de Árbol is a type of cayenne, most often found dried. Physical description: Skinny, tubular pod shape, usually starting to bend toward the tip; either red or green; 3 to 4 inches long.

SCOTCH BONNET (HABAÑERO): This is it. Generally acknowledged as the hottest commercially available chile pepper in the world, this baby, with all its Scoville rating of up to 300,000, will take you places you've never been before. Go ahead, laugh, but you won't be laughing after you get ahold of one of these.

Grown in Belize, many of the islands of the West Indies, and the Yucatán of Mexico, this is not an easy pepper to find. Your best bet is to try West Indian or Latin markets, where it can sometimes be located. Physical description: Lantern-shaped, short, fat, and slightly wrinkled (as its West Indian name suggests, it looks somewhat like a Scotsman's bonnet); yellow, red-orange, or green; 1 to 1½ inches long and about 1 inch in diameter.

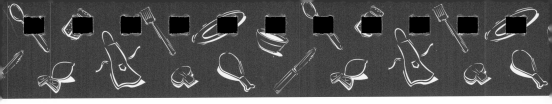

Sources

Unusual Ingredients

This list of places will enable you to get some of the harder-to-find ingredients used in this book. They are listed alphabetically by city within each category, and mail-order sources are indicated by an (*). Many of these stores also have catalogues they will send you, which is fun because then you can browse through the pages of exotic foreign ingredients.

General Ingredients

These four stores have a huge selection of ingredients, both fresh and prepared, from all over the culinary map. You can get a wide variety of ingredients from a single source if you so desire, and three have mail-order catalogues.

*RAFAL SPICE COMPANY
2521 Russell Street
Detroit, MI 48207
(800) 228-4276
In Michigan:
(313) 259-6373
(313) 259-6220 fax

*BALDUCCI'S
424 Sixth Avenue
New York, NY 10011
(212) 995-5065
Mail order:
1102 Queens Plaza
Long Island City, NY 11101
(800) 225-3822
(718) 786-4125 fax

*DEAN & DELUCA
560 Broadway
New York, NY 10012
(800) 781-4050
In New York:
(212) 226-6800

G. B. RATTO, INTERNATIONAL
GROCERS
821 Washington Street
Oakland, CA 94607
(510) 832-6503

Mexican/Latin American/Caribbean Ingredients

INDIA TEA AND SPICE, INC.
453 Common Street
Belmont, MA 02178
(617) 484-3737

TROPICAL FOODS, INC.
2101 Washington Street
Boston, MA 02119
(617) 442-9890

EL COLOSO MARKET
102 Columbia Street
Cambridge, MA 02139
(617) 491-1361

LA CASA DEL PUEBLO
1810 South Blue Island
Chicago, IL 60608
(312) 421-1417

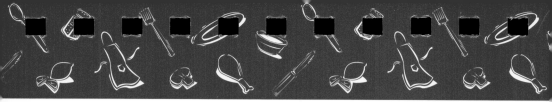

EL ORIGINAL SUPERMERCADO
CARDENAS
3922 North Sheridan Road
Chicago, IL 60607
(312) 525-5610

*LA PREFERIDA, INC.
3400 West 35th Street
Chicago, IL 60632
(312) 254-7200
(312) 254-8546 fax

HERNANDEZ MEXICAN FOODS
2120 Alamo Street
Dallas, TX 75202
(214) 742-2533

JOHNNIE'S MARKET
2030 Larimer Street
Denver, CO 80205
(303) 297-0155

ALGO ESPECIAL
2628 Bagley Street
Detroit, MI 48216
(313) 963-9013

LA COLMENA
2443 Bagley Street
Detroit, MI 48216
(313) 237-0295

HI-LO MARKET
415 Centre Street
Jamaica Plain, MA 02130
(617) 522-6364

THE GRAND CENTRAL MARKET
317 South Broadway
Los Angeles, CA
90013
(213) 622-1763

INTERNATIONAL GROCERIES AND
MEAT MARKET
5219 Ninth Avenue
(39th and 40th Streets)
New York, NY 10018
(212) 279-5514

CASA SANCHEZ
2778 24th Street
San Francisco, CA 94110
(415) 550-4463

AMERICANA GROCERY
1813 Columbia Road N.W.
Washington, DC 20009
(202) 265-7455

CASA PEÑA
1636 17th Street N.W.
Washington, DC 20009
(202) 462-2222

ASIAN INGREDIENTS

MING'S MARKET
1102-1108 Washington Street
Boston, MA 02118
(617) 426-8828

NEW ENGLAND FOOD
225 Harrison Avenue
Boston, MA 02111
(617) 426-8592

SUN SUN COMPANY
18 Oxford Street
Boston, MA 02111
(617) 426-6494

*STAR MARKET
3349 North Clark
Street, Chicago, IL 60657
(312) 472-0599
(312) 472-0599 fax

TAN VIET MARKET
10332 Ferguson Road
Dallas, TX 75228
(214) 324-5160

BANGKOK MARKET, INC.
4757 Melrose Avenue
Los Angeles, CA 90029
(213) 662-9705

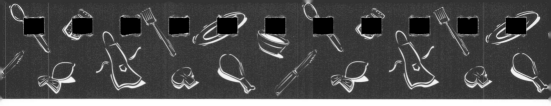

YEE SING CHONG COMPANY, INC.
988 North Hill
Los Angeles, CA 90012
(213) 626-9619

*SOUTHEASTERN FOOD SUPPLY
11077 NW 36th Avenue
Miami, FL 33167
(305) 688-2228
(305) 685-7500 fax

*KAM KUO FOOD CORPORATION
7 Mott Street
New York, NY 10013
(212) 349-3097
(212) 349-3097 fax

*KAM MAN FOOD PRODUCTS
200 Canal Street
New York, NY 10013
(212) 571-0330
(212) 766-9085 fax

*KATAGARI & COMPANY, INC.
(large Japanese selection)
224 East 59th Street
New York, NY 10022
(212) 755-3566
(212) 752-4197 fax

DA HUA MARKET
623 H Street N.W.
Washington, DC 20001
(202) 371-8888

GREEK AND MIDDLE EASTERN INGREDIENTS

SAHADI IMPORTING COMPANY, INC.
187 Atlantic Avenue
Brooklyn, NY 11201
(718) 624-4550

*C & K IMPORTING COMPANY
2771 West Pico Boulevard
Los Angeles, CA 90006
(213) 737-2970
(213) 737-3571 fax

INDIAN INGREDIENTS AND EXOTIC SPICES

INDIAN TEA & SPICES
453 Common Street
Belmont, MA 02178
(617) 484-3737

*BAZAAR OF INDIA
1810 University Avenue
Berkeley, CA 94703
(510) 548-4110
(510) 548-1115 fax

*HOUSE OF SPICES
82-80 Broadway
Jackson Heights, NY 11373
(718) 476-1577

MARKET SPICES
85A Pike Place Market
Seattle, WA 98101
(206) 622-6340

MISCELLANEOUS INGREDIENTS

GENUINE SMITHFIELD HAMS:
*Gwaltney, Inc.
P.O. Box 489
Smithfield, VA 23431
(804) 399-0417
Mail order:
P.O. Box 1
Smithfield, VA 23431
(800) 292-2773
(757) 357-0562 fax

A VARIETY OF HARDWOODS AND HARDWOOD CHARCOALS:

*DON HYSKO PEOPLE'S WOODS
75 Mill Street
Cumberland, RI 02864
(401) 725-2700
(800) 729-5800

HOT CHILE PEPPERS TO GROW YOURSELF:

THE PEPPER GAL, DOROTHY L. VAN VLECK
10536 119th Avenue North
Largo, FL 34643

ROSWELL SEED CO.
115–117 South Main
P.O. Box 725
Roswell, NM 88201
(505) 622-7701

LATIN VEGETABLES TO GROW YOURSELF:

J. A. MAKO HORTICULTURAL EXPERIENCE
P.O. Box 34082
Dallas, TX 75234

ASIAN VEGETABLES TO GROW YOURSELF:

MELLINGER'S
2310 West South Range Road
North Lima, OH 44452
(330) 549-9861
Mail order:
(800) 321-7444

FOR INNER BEAUTY HOT SAUCE:

LE SAUCIER
Faneuil Hall Market
Boston, MA 02109
(617) 227-9649

*DEAN & DELUCA
560 Broadway
New York, NY 10012
(212) 226-6800
(800) 781-4050

EAST COAST GRILL
1271 Cambridge Street
Cambridge, MA 02138
(617) 491-6568

The Pottery Barn's
catalog

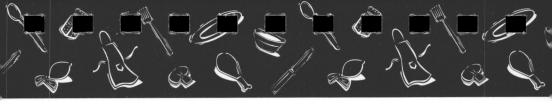

INDEX

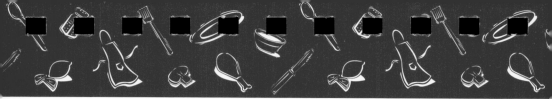

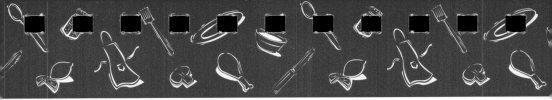

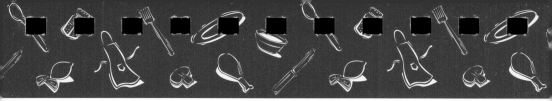